PUB WAL
IN
Exmoor & North Devon

THIRTY CIRCULAR WALKS
AROUND EXMOOR & NORTH DEVON INNS

Charles Whynne-Hammond

COUNTRYSIDE BOOKS
NEWBURY, BERKSHIRE

COUNTRYSIDE BOOKS
3 Catherine Road
Newbury, Berkshire

ISBN 1 85306 333 9

Cover illustration by Colin Doggett
Photographs by the author
Maps by Glenys Jones

Produced through MRM Associates Ltd., Reading
Typeset by Paragon Typesetters, Queensferry, Clwyd
Printed in England by J. W. Arrowsmith Ltd., Bristol

Contents

Introduction

Exmoor is well-known for its beauty. Its wild moorlands, wooded combes and undulating farmlands – not to mention its spectacular coastal scenery – have all meant that this area has become a popular holiday destination. But North Devon, away from these high landscapes, is not so famous. Neither is it so well visited. Yet it is a lovely area and, in its way, just as beautiful as its more notable neighbour. Between the great masses of Exmoor and Dartmoor, and throughout the region bordering North Cornwall, are vast areas of unspoilt countryside. Rolling hills are drained by great river systems – the Taw and Torridge especially – and wild undiscovered woodlands sweep over the contours. The population here is sparse and even the principal towns are small and intimate. The villages are quietly ancient; the farmsteads are scattered. Amongst the buildings there is an abundance of thatch, and cob walls are quite common.

I hope you find that the walks described in the book reflect the full variety of the Exmoor and North Devon landscape. The scenery is exciting and unexplored, but perfectly safe. The circular routes are not long by most walking standards, varying in length between two and five miles. Public footpaths are used most frequently, but bridleways, farm tracks, country lanes and 'permitted' paths are also used where necessary. All rights of way should be walkable and I have covered the routes described in this book personally without difficulty. But the terrain is never completely dry and vegetation can grow quickly. So a stout pair of outdoor shoes is an essential piece of equipment before setting out.

The Ordnance Survey Maps referred to in the book are from the 1:50,000 Landranger series. These show the features of the landscape on a scale most usually suitable for an average length walk. However, for those walks in the Exmoor area the OS Outdoor Leisure Map (1:25,000 scale) may also be used. This shows field boundaries, vegetation and various tourist facilities and may prove invaluable to the dedicated rambler.

Generally, pubs still keep 'normal' opening times – 11 am or 11.30 am to 2.30 pm lunchtimes, 6.30 pm or 7 pm to 11 pm evenings. These hours may be extended slightly on Saturdays and reduced slightly on Sundays. Variations in these times are given in the text. All the pubs listed are friendly and welcoming. Landlords are happy for customers to leave their vehicles in the pub car parks while they go for a short walk, but it would be polite for this to be arranged specifically on each occasion. Walkers should also be reminded that valuables should not be left visibly in their cars.

Nowadays the choice of food and drink offered by pubs is wide and varied. Most landlords serve a full range of snacks and meals, real ale and various wines and ciders. The items mentioned in the pub profiles are intended only to give an example of the choices on offer. They do not aim to give comprehensive lists. Vegetarians are generally well catered for, but any specific dietary requirement should be addressed to the landlords, who are usually only too happy to co-operate.

I should like to thank all those pub proprietors who supplied me with valuable information regarding their establishments. I am also indebted to Glenys Jones for drawing the maps and to Gwen Cassell who helped with the final draft. I hope you enjoy using this book as much as I did preparing it.

Charles Whynne-Hammond
Spring 1995

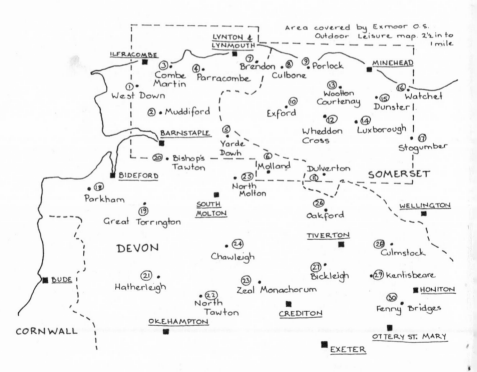

Area map shows location of walks.

How to behave when out walking is largely common sense, but it is always a good idea to remember the Country Code –

Enjoy the countryside and respect its life and work
Guard against all risk of fire
Fasten all gates
Keep your dogs under close control
Keep to public paths across farmland
Use gates and stiles to cross fences, hedges and walls
Leave livestock, crops and machinery alone
Take your litter home
Help to keep all water clean
Protect wildlife, plants and trees
Take special care on country roads
Make no unnecessary noise

Publisher's Note

We hope that you obtain considerable enjoyment from this book; great care has been taken in its preparation. However, changes of landlord and actual closures are sadly not uncommon. Likewise, although at the time of publication all routes followed public rights of way or permitted paths, diversion orders can be made and permissions withdrawn.

We cannot of course be held responsible for such diversion orders and any resultant inaccuracies in the text which result from these or any other changes to the routes nor any damage which might result from walkers trespassing on private property. We are anxious that all details covering the walks and the pubs are kept up to date and would therefore welcome information from readers which would be relevant to future editions.

1 West Down
The Crown Inn

This old, attractive and friendly pub suitably serves this old, attractive and friendly village. A happy local for happy locals! But everyone is equally welcome at the Crown, not just regulars but walkers and holidaymakers alike. There is a family room and, in the gardens, children's play equipment; pub games facilities are provided; teas and coffees are offered as well as the more usual pub drinks. The large and landscaped grounds behind the building are justifiably popular, for their lawns, shrubberies and pergola. In summer the place is a mass of flowers. The lounge is to the right as you enter, the public bar to the left. The latter is further sub-divided by screens into three sections, one containing the pool table, another the dartboard. All is cosy and comfortable. The walls are hung with a fun mixture of mementoes; horse-shoes, old farm implements, prints and even cartoons. Local posters are also pinned up.

The Crown Inn is a freehouse, serving real ales (like Flowers Original), draught cider (like Thatchers' Traditional) and selected wines. A full range of food is also on offer with bar snacks (including sandwiches and rolls) main meals (including steaks, trout, salmon and various salads) and vegetarian dishes (like non-meat lasagnes).

Everything, in fact, from burgers to bakes. Normal pub opening times are kept, slightly longer in the summer.

Telephone: 01271 862790.

How to get there: West Down is just 4 miles south of Ilfracombe, a little to the east of the A361 road to Braunton. Barnstaple is 7 miles away to the south-east. The village stands near the top of a narrow valley, on one of the upper tributaries of the river Caen. The Crown will be found near the centre of the village, close to the church.

Parking: There is a pub car park. Vehicles can also be left anywhere else in the village provided no obstruction is created. Drivers are asked to avoid those spaces specifically set aside for locals.

Length of the walk: 2½ miles. Map: OS Landranger sheet 180 Barnstaple and Ilfracombe (inn GR 516422).

There is lovely countryside hereabouts, with deep wooded combes and open hillside where sheep graze in large pasture fields edged by hedgerows. From the nearby summits you can see the sea, in the valleys you can study the flora and fauna of rural Devon. One popular walk is down the river Caen to Little Comfort, another is eastwards over the hills to Bittadon. The route suggested here offers an alternative; a gentle stroll up to Aylescott Lane and back. This lane follows the line of an old trackway linking Ilfracombe to Braunton. The footpaths used, crossing the farmland above West Down, are all well signposted and marked by numerous arrow discs.

The Walk

Just a few yards to the east of the Crown Inn is the small United Reformed Church, standing half-hidden behind some cottages. The route begins along the path that runs alongside that church, on its right-hand side. A footpath signpost points the way. The path – at first tarmac – curves right past some more cottages and then left, to run beside some back gardens to a stile at the far end. Here is the northern edge of West Down, and fields now stretch out ahead.

Following the direction indicated by the arrow disc, walk along by the hedge and then diagonally half-right, to reach another stile in the bottom corner (close to a barn). Across the next field, in the same direction, you descend into the shallow valley, through some damp meadow vegetation and across a little stream. On the far side walk up the next field, again at an angle. Aim to the left of a cottage. At the top of this field you will find a gate and, a few yards to its left, a stile. Climb over the latter. There are now three large fields to cross. By following the arrow discs on each stile, you walk diagonally across to the far

9

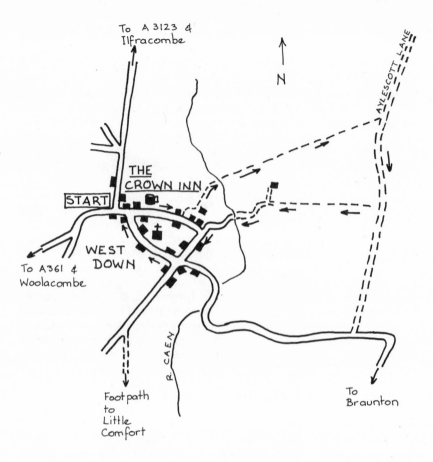

corner in each case. All this way you continue to climb and the views behind begin to open out. Across the third field you may choose to bear right along the field edge, owing to the nature of the cultivated field, but the right-of-way actually cuts across at an angle. You will find a stile half-hidden in the hedgerow.

At this point you reach the wide, stony trackway which is called Aylescott Lane. Turn right. This is a very pleasant stretch: straight hedgebanks on either side, full of wild flowers for much of the year, and sweeping hill scenery all around on the skyline. It is not difficult to imagine the trackway's former use as a dry ridgeway route for traders carrying goods inland from Ilfracombe's harbour. Drovers probably came this way too, driving their sheep and cattle to distant markets.

After about ¼ mile, when the trackway has descended a little and curved to the right a trifle, you will find two gates, one on either side facing each other. A footpath crosses at this point. Follow this to the right, over the stile a few yards away from the gate on that side. But leaving Aylescott Lane should not be too disappointing – it is a very pretty walk back to West Down across the fields. The route is clear all the way – and indeed, the village can be seen in the distance ahead for most of the journey.

As with the route out of West Down, the route back is clearly marked by arrow discs. Follow the edge of the first field (with the hedge on your right) and then cross the middle of the next field, negotiating a boggy rivulet on your way. Over the subsequent stile you continue in the same direction, climbing two further stiles and keeping West Down in front. In the bottom corner of the last field a gate leads through to a gravel track which curves down to the left. There is a ford across the stream here but an attractive stone footbridge can be used instead. A short ascent takes you back to the village, the church being reached by turning right.

West Down is well worth a wander round. Numerous old cottages, dating from the 17th century, cluster about the 13th century church, which itself boasts a fine interior with ancient bench-ends, memorials and stained glass. All the gardens seem to be well-kept, and planted with year-round colour, and the farm buildings give the necessary smell of the country. And should the Crown Inn be closed when you return, there is a conveniently placed tea shop opposite.

Muddiford
② The Muddiford Inn

This is a very popular place, with both locals and holidaymakers; and not surprisingly so. It is very friendly, very comfortable and offers a full range of refreshments. There is a separate restaurant, a family room and a large area outside where customers can sit on dry, sunny days. In short – this is the perfect pub.

Said to date back to the 15th century, the Muddiford Inn has a dark and cosy interior, with old beams and stone fireplaces. To the left of the main entrance is the public bar, with an area given over to darts, pool and shove-halfpenny. To the right is the lounge. There are settles and cushioned bench seats and the walls are hung with old prints. There is a separate entrance for the restaurant.

Being a Courage house it serves John Smith's real ale, together with a guest beer (like Webster's). Draught cider (Thatchers) and various house wines are also 'on tap'. But it is the choice of food that makes this pub so well-known. There is a full selection of bar snacks, from rolls upwards, and some delicious main course offerings, ranging from shepherd's pie, steak and old-fashioned casserole, to more exotic rice and pasta concoctions. All the meat is supplied by the local butcher.

Vegetarians are not forgotten and can choose such items as vegetable crumble and ratatouille.

Normal pub opening times are kept. Those planning an evening restaurant meal might be wise to book beforehand.

Telephone: 01271 850243.

How to get there: Muddiford nestles at the fringes of Exmoor, amongst the hills between Ilfracombe and Barnstaple, 6 miles from the former and 4 miles from the latter. Braunton is 5 miles away to the west. The village stands on the B3230 road, along the valley of Bradiford Water. The Muddiford Inn will be found on the eastern side of that road – on your right as you enter the village from the Barnstaple end.

Parking: There is a large pub car park, situated opposite the inn on the other side of the road. There are few other places where vehicles can be left, although a gravel lay-by does exist beside the lane to Higher Muddiford.

Length of the walk: 4 miles. Map: OS Landranger sheet 180 Barnstaple and Ilfracombe (inn GR 564383).

Hills, valleys, woods and farms: this is a landscape where the views are always changing, but the solitude remains the same. It is not a well walked part of Devon, even though the Exmoor National Park is just a few miles distant. But it is a beautiful, unspoilt part of Devon and deserves to be enjoyed.

The route involves footpaths across farmland, narrow country lanes and gravel trackways. Throughout, these ways are clearly signposted. However, because of lack of use some stretches of path may be a little overgrown.

The Walk

Turn right outside the Muddiford Inn and walk along the main road a short way, until the United Reformed chapel is reached, where you turn left. This is the lane to Higher Muddiford, which crosses a little stone bridge close by the junction. You will see the footpath signpost a little way down here on the right-hand side. Take the gravel track indicated, past a barn. This track soon becomes grassy, and not a little overgrown in springtime. A short way along here go through the gate on the left. Do not continue along the track, for it bends right and will take you back to the main road through the village.

For about ½ mile now you walk along the side of the valley, through a number of fields, towards Milltown which you can see in the distance ahead. The path is not clear but the route is easy to follow. Keep the river down to your right and the steep bracken-clad slope

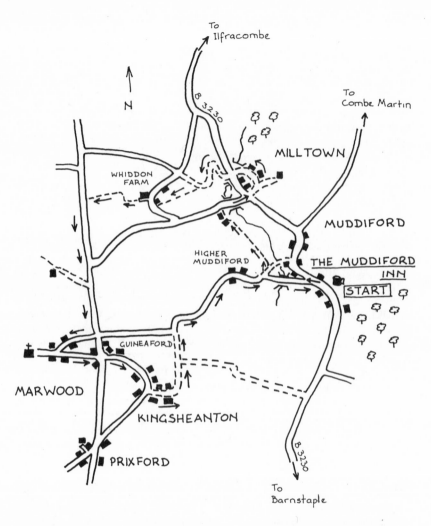

up to your left. Contour along thus, through each hedgerow and through the necessary gates and stiles. In due course you reach a barn, a gate leading onto a tarmac lane, and a house called 'Crockers'. Beyond the row of detached houses along here is the road, upon which you turn right to reach the main B3230. Go straight across, to walk up a tarmac drive (past a footpath signpost) and, almost immediately, left down an earthy track. This curves down through the back of Milltown, past some houses, until you reach the B3230 once again. Take the lane opposite, labelled as a 'No Through Road'.

14

The route now zig-zags up a steep slope, the lane bending first to the right and then to the left (at a cottage called 'The Thatch'). The surface becomes concrete, then gravel. In due course you swing to the right again, as you reach the upper portion of the valley side. On the left, half hidden by the hedgerow and before you reach a tall cedar tree, is a stile. This leads through to an open field, from where the views begin to open out. Aim for the farmstead down below in the valley, walking diagonally downhill keeping the large barn up to your right. There are gates to go through but the road should be reached without trouble. Turn right up this road and then left along a gravel track where stands a footpath signpost. This track leads through the centre of Whiddon Farm, with barns and cattle yards all round. Continue straight through, up a grassy track, keeping the tall silo tower to your right. At the next gate turn right (to keep the silo still to your right) and then, beyond the following gateway, left. A wide, earthy track now leads you directly, along the edge of a field, to the road at the top. Once on the road turn left.

For about the next mile you keep to the roads. But these are not normal roads. They are Devon minor roads: narrow, quiet lanes with high hedgerows either side. Enjoy the views and wild flowers. Walk south until you reach a junction of lanes, where you turn west (right) to Marwood. From there keep left, to reach Guineaford and then straight on (across that junction) to Kingsheanton. In this way you will be able to enjoy three extremely pretty hamlets. Marwood is especially attractive, with a 14th century church (complete with old sundial), a classical style manor house and gardens which are open to the public. Depending on the season these gardens are a riot of colour, with roses, rhododendrons, camellias and all manner of flowering shrubs.

From Kingsheanton take the lane marked as a dead end, leading uphill at the eastern end of the village. Soon the tarmac gives way to gravel and earth, climbing all the while. Towards the top a private track continues uphill, but the bridleway (for such this trackway is) swings left, to begin a gradual descent. This is a pleasant section. The ground underfoot is firm, the way is well-marked by hedgerows, and there are views all around. Keeping to this main, wide track, as it dips a little and then climbs again (and ignoring another track off to the right) you will eventually meet a road. Turn right and follow this as it bends right itself to descend steeply to Higher Muddiford. Muddiford proper, and its inn, stand at the bottom of a further steep descent, down in the bottom of the valley.

3 Combe Martin
The Pack of Cards

Unique is an over-used word, but it does apply to this particular pub. It was built in the late 17th century by a certain George Ley following a lucky win at the gambling tables. Its design resembles that of a 'fairytale' castle and its features originally represented the numbers in a pack of cards. There were four floors, 52 windows, 13 rooms and – according to local tradition – the whole building stood on a 52 ft square site. From being a private home it became an inn some time in the early 19th century.

Today the Pack of Cards offers friendliness, hospitality and an excellent range of refreshments. Overnight accommodation is available; there is a bar, a restaurant and a large riverside garden where children's play equipment is laid out; cream teas as well as bar snacks and main meals are served; and the place is open all day from 11 am to 11 pm.

Through the conservatory, approached from the garden, is the central hall where stags' antlers and old farm implements share the wall-space with the blackboards where the menus are written. To one side is the large bar room, to the other is the dining room. The decor is cosy and comfortable and the decoration has links with playing cards – naturally. As a freehouse, a number of real ales are offered (including Bass and Directors), various draught ciders and house wines. The choice of food is excellent, ranging from snacks like ploughman's lunches, sandwiches, jacket potatoes and salads to meals like steak, chicken and fish dishes. 'Sweet and sour' items are a speciality and there is always a choice for vegetarians.

The Pack of Cards may be a folly – and one now protected as an Ancient Monument – but going there to eat and drink would be anything but foolish!

Telephone: 01271 882300.

How to get there: Combe Martin is a well-known holiday resort 3 miles along the coast, eastwards from the even more well-known Ilfracombe. It is 10 miles north of Barnstaple. The town stands on the western edge of the Exmoor National Park and provides a perfect base from which to explore that area. The Pack of Cards will be found about half-way along the main road through town, on the western side a little north from the church.

Parking: There is a large pub car park. There is also a large public car park at the bottom end of the town, close to the quay.

Length of the walk: 4½ miles. Map: OS Landranger sheet 180 Barnstaple and Ilfracombe (inn GR 583467).

From Combe Martin the South-West Coast Long Distance Footpath can be explored in both directions. Each way the cliff scenery is breathtaking and, on clear days, the view northwards is across the Bristol Channel to Wales. The walk westwards to Ilfracombe is popular since it passes many holiday sites and Watermouth Castle, which is a children's fun centre. This walk is eastwards, along a stretch of coast that is quieter, higher and more rugged.

The route is by way of Little Hangman to Great Hangman, the high cliff where vast, panoramic views are offered, returning more inland via the farmlands of Challacombe. All the paths are very clear but there are inevitably some steep climbs.

The Walk
To reach the sea turn left outside the Pack of Cards and walk down the main street of the town. Combe Martin is essentially a one-street town, along the A399 which runs along the bottom of the valley. This is a narrow valley and the wooded slopes on either side are very close. Towards the bottom end bear right, at a fork, along Cross Street. This leads to the tourist information office, the public car park and – the most attractive part of town – the little harbour. There is also a beach here that can be very large at low tide.

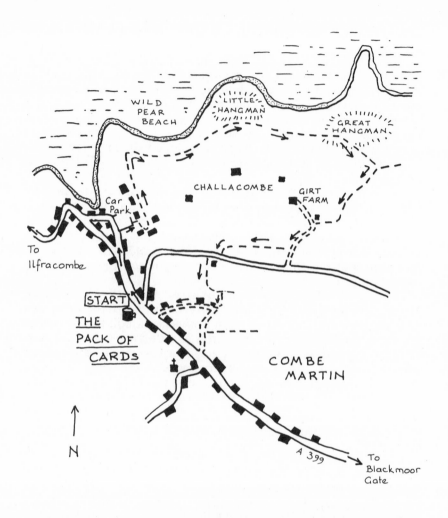

The coastal path eastwards is well signposted. You could reach it by ascending the cliff steps that rise from the sands beyond the quay. But an easier route lies through the car park. A footpath signpost at the top points the way between houses. The path bends right, then left, to climb up a rough flight of steps. After running behind a line of houses it then turns right (at a T-junction) to pass a wooden shelter. By this time you have left Combe Martin behind and you are on the cliffs. Simply continue and enjoy the exhilarating views.

The coastal footpath route, of course, needs little guidance. At the beginning are signs to Lester Point and the Hangmans, and all the way along the very clear track leads you across the grassy slopes of the clifftops. Apart from an early descent, into the valley that leads to Wild Pear Beach, the way is uphill. There are some stiles to climb but at no point does the footpath come anywhere near the cliff edge.

Little Hangman is the first summit to conquer. It is a splendid, conical-shaped clifftop that seems very high from below. It will later seem very low, when viewed from Great Hangman. You could, in fact, bypass this summit by keeping to its southern slopes (landward side) and continuing on the coastal path along by the stone wall. But why miss this little sense of achievement? And the views from the top are splendid.

The long ascent to Great Hangman, interrupted by a kissing-gate and, later, by a stile, is even more worthwhile. From the top of this – a point marked by a rough cairn – the panorama is spectacular: the coastline of Exmoor, the rolling hills inland across North Devon, the uplands of Wales (on clear days) across the Severn Sea. In summer the moorland clifftop is ablaze with colour – heather and gorse flowering in profusion.

The journey back begins down the coast path away from Combe Martin. This leads down towards Sherrycombe, a shallow valley east of Great Hangman. Soon you reach a stone wall. Follow the path to the right signposted to Combe Martin and County Road. This runs inland to a gate and stile and thence along the edge of a field to another gate. Beyond this a gravel track continues in the same direction, running between stone walls. In due course this track bends right and descends to a gate, past a cottage. Ignoring the lane to Girt Farm keep left, as the track curves up out of the combe. Just 200 yards further on, turn right along a much narrower, grassy track that runs between hedgerows.

This is a pretty stretch, since the view to the right takes in the sea, Little Hangman and, down below, the Challacombe farmsteads. In due course you descend steeply, through the bushes, to a tarmac lane. Turn right downhill. You could simply continue along this lane, for it leads directly back to Combe Martin. But a more interesting route involves footpaths. About 10 yards down on the left, immediately after Silver Dale Nurseries, turn left along a grassy track between hedges. This is a dark and narrow way, going steeply downhill. Halfway down it turns sharply right to continue the descent. At the bottom there is an old barn on the right. The way now becomes much wider, and gravel-floored. Keeping to the right the track curves several times as it runs below the trees and between some large detached houses. It becomes a tarmac lane (now called Chapel Lane) and emerges onto the main road. The Pack of Cards will be seen down to your right, hardly a stone's throw away.

Parracombe
The Fox and Goose Inne

This Victorian building replaces an older, thatched one that was destroyed by fire towards the end of the 19th century. In former times this pub was part of the Blackmore estate, and linked to the family of R.D. Blackmore, who wrote *Lorna Doone*.

Today the Victorian character remains. Inside there are high, wood-panelled ceilings, plain walls hung with old pictures and traditional furniture. There is one main bar room, which acts as a lounge, and an almost separate area dominated by a pool table, which acts as a public bar. To the right of the hallway, as you enter, is a quiet little dining room. The Fox and Goose offers bed and breakfast accommodation and there can be few more pleasant places to stay.

This freehouse serves real ales, including Boddingtons and Flowers Original, and Addlestone's cider. The range of food on offer is excellent, this being listed on menu cards with daily specials written up on blackboards. Bar snacks can be sandwiches, jacket potatoes and salads, main meals can be chicken, sausages, pasties, burgers, fish dishes and chilli con carne. There is a special menu for children and vegetarians can choose such items as cheese and leek bake or courgette and mushroom lasagne. Evening meals are different, with a slight bias towards poultry, although the 'nut paella' looks very good. This is a friendly pub where families are welcome. Locals and tourists mix happily and, in winter, an open fire adds to the cosiness. Telephone: 01598 763239.

How to get there: Parracombe is not on a main road, but is bypassed by the A39 as it runs between Lynton and Blackmore Gate, which are 5 miles and 2 miles away respectively. Combe Martin is 5 miles to the west. The Fox and Goose will be found at the western end of the village, at the bottom of the hill, below the church.

Parking: There is a pub car park on the opposite side of the road. Elsewhere in the village there are not many other places where vehicles can be left, the lanes being steep, winding and narrow.

Length of the walk: 2½ miles. Map: OS Landranger sheet 180 Barnstaple and Ilfracombe (inn GR 667448).

Parracombe nestles in hilly country, towards the top end of the Heddon valley, a wooded combe well-known for its beauty. There are many footpaths running down this valley offering several options for circular walks.

This route, however, circles the landscape upstream from Parracombe, skirting the tributaries that feed the headwaters of the river Heddon. The route also includes the old church (now redundant but preserved) which stands up at Churchtown. This beautiful little building was superseded when the Victorians erected the 'new church' down in the village centre. For most of the circuit clear bridleways are used, so there should be no problems about path-finding. Generally, the ground underfoot is firm, except where horses' hooves have churned the earth.

The Walk

To reach Churchtown, about ½ mile away, turn left outside the Fox and Goose and then right at the telephone box some few yards away. This lane leads uphill and is signposted to the village hall. The 'new church' – that is, the one built in 1878 – will be seen on the left, surrounded by its sloping graveyard. As you climb, bear right at the junction to follow the signs pointing to Churchtown. This bends at Sunnyside Farm, further up, and leads up below the trees out of the village. At the top the lane ends and a gravel track proceeds, right, across a stone bridge that once crossed a railway line. Ahead are tea gardens and a sign pointing to a walk along the old railway track, both of which you may enjoy another time. For now, however, continue along the gravel track. Round the corner is St Petrock's church.

This, known as the 'old church', is 11th century and has fortunately been preserved by the Redundant Churches Fund. It is a lovely little

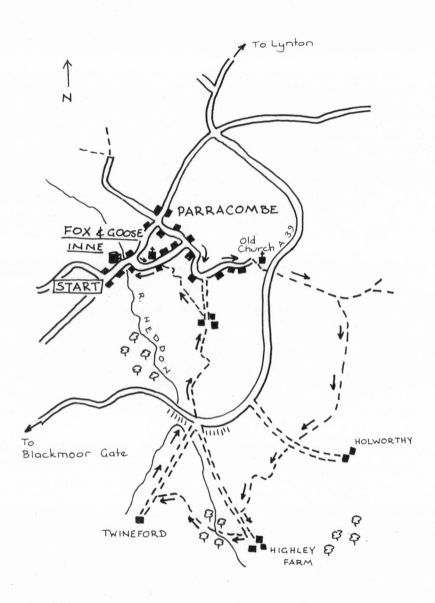

To Lynton

N

PARRACOMBE

FOX & GOOSE
INNE

Old
Church

A 39

START

R. HEDDON

HOLWORTHY

To
Blackmoor Gate

TWINEFORD

HIGHLEY
FARM

building, with an undamaged interior of box pews, pulpit, screen and desks dating from the 17th and 18th centuries. When the Victorians were erecting their new church they were going to demolish this little gem, until John Ruskin (the famous critic and arbiter of taste) stepped in. He organised a protest and won the building's reprieve. In fact, this part of Parracombe would be pleasant even without its church. There are views across the rest of the village, and down the Heddon valley, and the old railway line makes for an idyllic wildlife corridor. Here ran the Lynton and Barnstaple railway, a two-foot gauge miniature railway opened in 1898 as a tourist line. Despite the scenic quality of its route it never became financially viable and closed in 1936.

The circular walk continues along the gravel track (keeping left at the fork) to the main A39 road a couple of hundred yards further on. Cross this and continue on the far side along a clear gravel track with a bridleway signpost pointing to Parracombe Common. This curves up to reach two farm gates. Go through the one on the right.

The route now continues along a grassy track between hedgerows. There are views all around. After the next gate the track begins to descend and beyond the following gate you continue along the bottom edge of a field to reach a gravel farm track. Through more gates cross over this track into the next field and follow the hedgerow round to reach the top of a rutted trackway which you take down into the valley. At the bottom you meet a clearer farm track, that leads you left towards Highley Farm, crossing the stream as you go. Just before the farmyard turn sharply right, to go through a gate onto a gravel track. This climbs out of the valley between hedgerows, opening out into the fields at the crest. Through the gate on the right, at the top corner, continue in the same direction, keeping the valley (in fact, that of the Upper Heddon river) down to your right. In the following field bear half-left across the undulating grass to join a main trackway. Turn right and follow this to the road – the A39 again. This is embanked at the point where you join it, so the trackway zig-zags up right then left.

The footpath back to Parracombe is now clear enough, as it crosses a number of fields. A footpath over the first field is signposted on the far side of the A39. After contouring across this first field cross the second diagonally to a gate in the bottom corner. Beyond this follow a track for about 100 yards before turning left, through a gate. Keeping to the field edge you cross the stile and rivulet on the far side and continue up the next field to join a hedgerow. This leads you on to a gate, a trackway and, in due course, to the farm buildings. At the far side of the farmyard, and beyond the barn on the left, leave the farm track, through a gate also on the left. You will now see Parracombe 'new church' clearly ahead. Aim for this. In the bottom corner you enter the next field, cross the stream by stepping stones, and proceed to the left. A stile half-hidden by the hedgerow takes you onto the road, opposite the churchyard. Turn left for the Fox and Goose.

Yarde Down
5 The Poltimore Arms

This is a well-known pub, mentioned in many a guidebook as being a place which should serve as a good example to other establishments. The atmosphere is cosy and old-fashioned, the decor is rustic and comfortable, the welcome is genuine. It is a country pub in the very best tradition.

There are three small rooms inside: the main bar where the serving hatch forms the focal point; the dining room which is quieter and the place where families tend to sit; and, beyond the latter, the games room which includes a pool table. There are low ceilings with beams, large fireplaces, and plain walls hung with pictures of hunting scenes and local cricket teams. Stags' horns and brassware also decorate the rooms. The furniture is of the old wood and settle variety. Outside there is a pleasant garden, which proves very popular during summer weekends.

The Poltimore Arms is a freehouse and keeps normal pub opening times. Real ales are served (including Cotleigh and John Smith's) together with various wines and ciders. The quality and variety of the food is excellent – as would be expected at such a popular pub. Numerous tasty bar snacks are available lunchtimes (ploughman's, sandwiches, soups and so on) and in the evenings, main meals are served that would not be out of place in a good restaurant. There are grills, pies, casseroles, fish dishes, vegetable bakes, rice and pasta concoctions, and numerous tempting desserts. Carnivores and vegetarians alike will be amply satisfied.

Telephone: 01598 710381.

How to get there: The Poltimore Arms stands on the hillside above the hamlet of Yarde. To the north are some of the wildest and most remote parts of Exmoor – The Chains are just 4 miles away. The village of Simonsbath is 4 miles north-eastwards. The pub is most easily reached from the A399 Combe Martin to South Molton road, turning off at the village of Brayford.

Parking: Cars can be parked outside the pub, on a large forecourt. Elsewhere space may be limited owing to the narrowness of the country lanes here. However, vehicles can be left round the corner, where Sherracombe Lane begins.

Length of the walk: 4½ miles. Map: OS Landranger sheet 180 Barnstaple and Ilfracombe (inn GR 725356).

This splendid walk is well signposted throughout, the National Parks Authority having done a good job of erecting numerous pointer posts. Much of the route is along clear trackways, the rest is along footpaths across moorland pasture fields. There are a few stiles to climb but no obstacle hinders the pleasure of the ramble.

Wide views are to be enjoyed – towards the heather and gorse clad slopes of high Exmoor in one direction, and towards the unspoilt farmlands of North Devon in the other. There are, also, narrow, wooded combes to be seen and varied moorland wildlife.

The Walk
Turn left outside the Poltimore Arms, left again along the road to Simonsbath and left once more along the gravel trackway marked by a footpath signpost. The route is to Kedworthy and Whitefield. This is a wide shingle-floored track (known locally as Sherracombe Lane) and is a popular route to the open moor. You will be coming back this way at the end of your walk, so you have two opportunities to enjoy the views from here. And splendid are these views too – especially south-westwards across the Bray valley towards Barnstaple.

In due course the gravel surface ends (as it curves left into a field) and a grassy surface begins as the track continues its journey to the moors. It bends right, dips a little and runs alongside a woodland. Down beyond a gate you reach a spot called Sherracombe Ford,

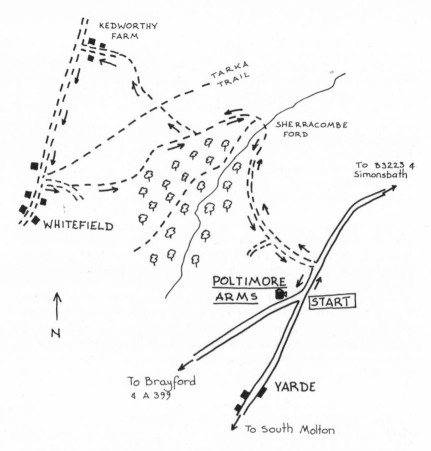

where the track swings left to cross the stream at the head of a wooded combe. What a pleasant spot this is! Follow the path round as it climbs the far side, walking uphill to a gate at the top. A footpath signpost, close to the ford, points the way to Kedworthy and Whitefield. It is to Kedworthy, in fact, that you are walking, so this is the name you should be looking for on the signposts.

Beyond the gate at the top of the slope there is another gate and a choice of routes. Do not go through that gate and follow the way that leads to the valley below. This is the path you will be returning along, later in the circuit. Instead, bear right and follow the fence uphill to another gate on the skyline. At that point you cross over the Tarka Trail – a long distance footpath across North Devon designated by the County Council and inspired by the famous otter story written by Henry Williamson. Continue in the same direction as before, still keeping the fence to your left-hand side. You will reach a gate at the brow of the hill, by which time there are views to be enjoyed ahead, north-westwards towards Challacombe.

Across the next field aim diagonally, half-right, until you join a track in the far corner. Now follow this downhill to Kedworthy Farm. There you continue past the farm buildings to reach a T-junction of tracks at the far side. Turn left, away from Muxworthy, which is signposted to the right. A long, concrete farm track now leads you all the way to Whitefield hamlet, where you begin the return journey to Yarde Down.

Just beyond the house called Winsley the Tarka Trail is signposted going off to the left, towards Moles Chamber. About 50 yards further on another footpath signpost points left to Sherracombe Ford. This is the route to follow. A gravel track leads you away from Whitefield hamlet to a gate. Through this, strike across the field diagonally half-left, crossing a small stream as you leave the gravel track. Aiming for Whitefield Down, which rises like a green dome on the skyline ahead, you cross two fields and go through two gates. Thereafter bear half-left as you descend to the woodland in the valley. Now keep this woodland to your right as you walk up the line of the valley, bearing right at the point where the trees end. Cross the grassy slope to the top end of the next finger of woodland. There you will find a gate to be recognised. You were at this point earlier. Bear right to descend the slope to Sherracombe Ford. From here you can return to the Poltimore Arms by way of Sherracombe Lane, retracing your first steps.

Good walk - one 'boggy bit'. Some steep climbs so quite tiring - Do not attempt if weather has been wet.

6 Molland
The London Inn

If only more village pubs were like this! The decor is rustic and old-fashioned, the food is home-cooked and imaginative, the friendliness is real and unaffected. And the setting is superb. The London Inn is a 15th century building set amidst a small attractive garden, at the centre of a beautiful, unspoilt village on the edge of Exmoor.

This is a long building sub-divided inside into a number of small, dark, cosy rooms. Through a front porch, where you can sit, is a public bar with dartboard. To the left, in the central area, is the bar counter itself in its own little room. Beyond this, at the far end, is the lounge, complete with piano. All around there are bare stone walls, low beams, wooden settle furniture and old pictures hung about the walls. The stone floors, the barrels ranged behind the bar counter, the hatch from the public bar to the serving area, all accentuate the feeling that you have gone back in time.

As a freehouse the London Inn sells a changing range of real ales, like Worthington Best and Bass, and draught ciders, like Blackthorn and local scrumpy. But it is the food that brings in the customers from far and wide. Apart from the usual fare of bar snacks (like ploughman's lunches, jacket potatoes, things with chips); and main meals (like fish, curry and salads); there are also specials using local produce – game pie for instance or trout. Supplementing the menu books kept on the counter, daily items are written up on a blackboard: a prawn provençale is a typical example.

Normal pub opening times are kept.

Telephone: 01769 550269.

How to get there: Molland is hidden amongst the hills of southern Exmoor, some 7 miles west of Dulverton. South Molton is 6 miles away to the south west, Tiverton is about 15 miles to the south east. The village does not stand on a main road but can be reached from the A361, turning along the B3227 road in the Bampton direction from near South Molton and then northwards from Combsland Cross. The London Inn will be found immediately west of Molland church.

Parking: There is sufficient car parking space outside the pub, in front of the church. Vehicles can also be left, here and there, throughout the village, where space allows.

Length of the walk: 4 miles. Map: OS Landranger sheet 181 Minehead and Brendon Hills (inn GR 807284).

This walk includes both farmland and moorland scenery, and offers wide-ranging views across North Devon as well as more intimate views over little wooded combes. The route crosses two small valleys by footpath to reach the edge of Molland Common (an open moor of heather, gorse and bracken). It returns via farm tracks and lanes. The way is clear throughout. Here and there the ground is liable to be muddy, after periods of wet weather, but this is normal in a district where horse-riding is popular. Hooves churn up the bridleways somewhat.

The Walk

The path to be taken runs up behind both the London Inn and the church, and begins immediately west of the pub. It starts as a gravel track, bearing right past a line of cottages and a farm. Beyond the latter it becomes a faint grassy way, running over the farmland. Cross diagonally, away from Molland, through two fields and two gates, after which you should find yourself on the road. This is Moor Lane, and it leads north to the open moorland. You do not follow this, however. Instead go straight over, and through a gate into another field. Now continue in the same direction as before. Be sure to look behind, for the views have opened out.

The path goes up, then down into a little, steep-sided combe, bearing slightly left as it descends. After following the little stream up

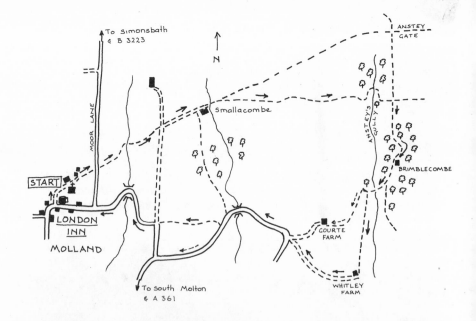

the valley for a short way it crosses over to the far side, by way of stepping stones, beneath some trees. You now continue up the steep grassy slope ahead, curving slightly left as you round the corner of a hedgerow. Beyond, diagonally in the far corner, a gate in the distant hedge leads out to a farm track. Proceed along this farm track eastwards, taking care to follow the one surfaced with tarmac and not the one, leading off to the left, surfaced with gravel. Incidentally, this tarmac track forms the boundary of the Exmoor National Park – and indeed, you will be running along this boundary for the next 1½ miles of the route.

Soon, near Smallacombe, you will see a bridleway signpost pointing right and another signpost showing that Anstey Gate is straight on. Follow the latter, the track continuing down to a gate, a ford and then up the other side onto the open moorland. By this time the track has become gravel but it is clear nonetheless. At the next signpost turn right, in the direction of West Anstey. Straight on would be the way to Anstey Gate, to be used by those walkers wishing to see Hawkridge or distant Dulverton.

For the next mile or so the walk is superb. The wide, grassy track heads eastwards, with the windswept heather and gorse to the left and the farmland, hemmed by stone hedgebanks, to the right. On the far horizon to the south are the red hills of mid-Devon. In due course you reach Anstey's Gully, at which point the track descends through the trees to cross the stream, bearing right as it ascends the other side. What an excellent picnic spot this would make: a sheltered, wooded combe at the edge of the moors.

After emerging from the trees, having climbed out of this combe, turn right, across a cattle grid. There is also a track continuing straight on, and another to the left but you ignore these. The track you want heads south along the edge of a field, with the view towards Dartmoor ahead. This grassy, stony way leads downhill to a wooded combe where it curves left, then right, to Brimblecombe Farm. There, you keep right, still descending through the trees. This is a lovely stretch, and should not be rushed. Towards the bottom ignore a path leading left to cross the valley and continue along the path straight ahead, as it keeps to the valley side. Over a little tributary stream you soon reach a gate. On the far side of this a choice of routes presents itself. Either bear right, to climb steeply uphill, or bear left to continue along the valley before climbing more gently up the valley side at an angle. The first option will take you over a hill spur to Gourte Farm and then to the road. The latter will take you through the gardens of Whitley Farm (after turning right through a gate at the top of your climb) and thence to the road along a gravel drive. The two routes meet at the road. The former is shorter but involves steeper slopes. The latter, is, perhaps, the prettier.

The route back to Molland is now easy. You can keep to the road the whole way: turn right when you reach the road and follow it westwards as it curves up and down, and round, two little combes. Alternatively you can cut off the second and longest curve by taking a footpath that runs along the edges of three fields. You can pick this up beyond the first combe, through a gate on the right as you reach the top of the slope. Either way the London Inn is now only ½ mile away.

7 **Brendon**
The Stag Hunters Hotel

In the early 19th century this was known as the Abbey Tavern, for the site was once occupied by a religious establishment. Monks in the Middle Ages tilled the valley hereabouts and fished the streams. Remnants of their old chapel can be seen in the Abbey Lounge – said to be the most ancient building in the Brendon valley.

Today the Stag Hunters happily combines the functions of a luxurious country hotel with the atmosphere of a traditional village inn. At the pub end there are two large bar rooms, a lounge and public bar. There are low, beamed ceilings, bare stone fireplaces and wooden bench-style furniture. The beams in the public bar have been written upon, commemorating various groups and customers who have enjoyed their time here.

This is certainly the sort of place where people would enjoy themselves. It is open all day, from 11 am to 11 pm, and serves a wonderful range of food. There are home-made soups, ploughman's lunches and other such traditional snacks; there are meat pies, steaks, seafood platters and fish dishes – all listed on the regular menu. But it is the local dishes, and the daily specials, that are especially good: Exmoor lamb, pheasant, rabbit and venison, locally-caught trout or farm duck. And the vegetable chilli would certainly tempt the vegetarians.

This is a freehouse, serving such real ales as Tetley and Butcombe. Copperhead draught cider and various wines are also listed. The garden, which is across the road, overlooks the river.

Telephone: 015987 222.

How to get there: Brendon is situated in the valley of the East Lyn river, just 3 miles east of Lynton and Lynmouth. It stands 1 mile south of the A39 road to Porlock, which is 8 miles to the east. The Stag Hunters Hotel will be found a little to the west of the bridge over the river.

Parking: There is a pub car park to one side. Vehicles may also be left here and there throughout the village, where space permits.

Length of the walk: 4½ miles. Map: OS Landranger sheet 180 Barnstaple and Ilfracombe (inn GR 767482).

There are many excellent circular walks from Brendon, of various distances and offering several different kinds of scenery. The walk westwards along the East Lyn river to Watersmeet is very popular, returning by way of Wilsham. The walk northwards to Foreland Point, thence along the coastal footpath, is also pleasant, this including a visit to a Roman fort at Old Barrow Hill.

This circular walk is eastwards to Malmsmead and back, along each side of the East Lyn valley. The views here are excellent, especially through Ashton Cleave, where the valley is steep-sided and wooded. Malmsmead – a local tourist 'honeypot' – is the gateway to Doone country since it stands at the northern end of Badgworthy Water. All the paths are very clear and distinct, but there are several climbs as well.

The Walk

Leaving the Stag Hunters Hotel in an easterly direction walk past the post office and turn left to cross the bridge over East Lyn river. On the far side turn right to walk up the lane that, in due course, bears left past some cottages. Just around this bend, on the right, is a footpath signpost, pointing to a tall step-stile. This reads 'County Gate, Malmsmead via Ashton Cleave'. It is the way you want.

A steep climb awaits you, up a grassy slope covered with moorland vegetation. But the way is very clear and is marked by wooden waymarker posts. The path curves its way towards the top, in due course reaching a pedestrian gate. Beyond this the ascent slackens and the path begins to contour. Above it, to the left, is the farmland; below it to the right are the gorsy, heathery slopes of the valley side.

This popular, well-trodden footpath along the East Lyn valley needs

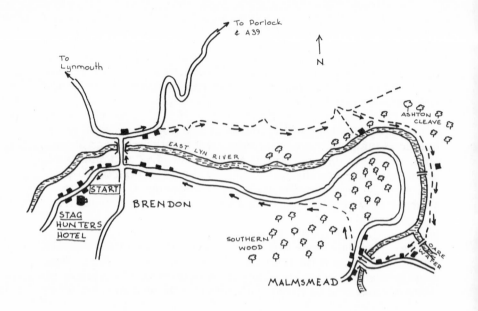

little description. There is one stretch, beyond a gate, that climbs and there is a later stretch, before another gate, that descends but essentially this is a level walk. The contours are followed. The views, all the way, are super and the ground is firm underfoot. In due course you reach a side combe, where the path curves and dips to cross a tributary stream by a stile and footbridge. On the far side of this, turn left, to go uphill a little before bearing right again to resume your original direction. On the far side of the pedestrian gate (not the farm gate you first reach on your left) is a fork and footpath signpost. The left fork climbs towards County Gate. The right fork descends towards Malmsmead and Oare. Take the latter direction, but not before you have gasped at the view of Ashton Cleave.

A fairly steep descent now takes you down through the heather, gorse and bracken to the East Lyn riverbank. This you now follow, over a stile and along a wide grassy path running beneath the trees. This is a lovely section, and should not be rushed. The river, the trees, the meadows: the ensemble is perfect for a quiet stroll. Ignoring the first footbridge you come to, close to Glebe Farm, cross the stream by the second, an attractive curved structure with steps at either end. At the other side continue along a track, until you reach Parsonage Farm, beyond which is the road. Turn right to go downhill to Malmsmead.

This is an interesting, attractive hamlet – but not an undiscovered one. For it acts as a gateway to *Lorna Doone* country and many tourists come here to visit the gift, garden and refreshment shops, to park their cars in the large car park, to eat at the picnic site, to use the public conveniences and to photograph the old stone bridge over the river. Up the road a little is the Exmoor Natural History Society Centre where interesting displays teach about local wildlife. When all the visitors have gone this is, indeed, a pleasant spot.

The journey back to Brendon begins at the right-hand end of the barn opposite the bridge. The bridleway sign (to Malmsmead Hill and Brendon Common) is almost opposite the car park and the track leads up at an angle, through a gate. Another gate, further uphill, leads through to the woodlands. This is Southern Wood, a pleasant, deciduous wood, surprisingly quiet considering its proximity to Malmsmead. The path – a clear trackway – leads up below the trees, curves left and then descends eventually to meet a tarmac lane. Turn left along this lane, for it will take you back to the Stag Hunters Hotel. It is a narrow, quiet lane that follows the south side of the East Lyn valley. You follow it for almost a mile but few vehicles should pass. And the scenery should be enjoyed without much disturbance. So take your time and be happy with a good walk well accomplished.

Culbone
8

The Culbone Inn

This advertises itself as the 'highest free house on Exmoor' – and certainly its position is enviable. There are views far southward, towards the slopes above Simonsbath, and down below are the wooded combes that wind round to the Doone country. There is no village here, only a meeting of roads and bridleways.

Once a post house, the Culbone Inn still offers hospitality and refreshment. Accommodation is available and, since the place opens for slightly longer than normal pub opening times, morning coffee is served as well as alcoholic and soft drinks. Real ales include Bass and another brewed especially for the establishment. Draught cider and various wines are also served.

Inside there is one main bar room, decorated traditionally with dark wood furniture and plain walls hung with bird prints. Along one side is a large, bare-stone fireplace – a focal point in winter when the logs are ablaze. Orders for coffee and food are taken at the bar counter at the far end.

And the food is very good indeed. The regular menu includes soups, sandwiches, ploughman's lunches, salads and curries, whilst the daily specials (written up on a board at the counter) might include fish and pasta dishes or vegetarian bakes. Indeed, there is always a choice of food for vegetarians, as well as for those who see eating as a health-and-fitness exercise.

This is a friendly, happy pub where the staff are ever-willing to discuss life up here in the wilds of Exmoor.

Telephone: 01643 862259.

How to get there: Culbone Hill stands between Lynton and Porlock, being one of the highest points along the Exmoor coastline. The inn is situated on the A39 main road, on the left (south side) as you aproach from Porlock Hill, some 3 miles away. The pub can also be approached from Exford, along the moorland road that crosses Wilmersham Common.

Parking: The Culbone Inn has its own large car park. Vehicles should not be left along the side of the A39, but can be parked along the lane opposite, which goes to Culbone church. A large parking area will be found near the cattle grid, some 200 yards up.

Length of the walk: 4½ miles. Map: OS Landranger sheet 181 Minehead and Brendon Hills (inn GR 830472).

The Culbone Inn is popular with walkers, for it is well placed between the footpaths along the coast and those which run inland towards Doone country. Culbone church, the smallest parish church in England, is half hidden amongst woodlands, overlooking the sea 2 miles north of the pub. It can be reached by way of the coastal footpath.

This walk offers a circuit into that area made famous by RD Blackmore, in his novel 'Lorna Doone'. It follows the valley of Oare Water from Robber's Bridge to Oare church. Clear footpaths are used, and one stretch of very quiet country lane.

The Walk

The track to Robber's Bridge – in fact, a bridleway signposted to Oareford, 1½ miles – begins opposite the lane to Culbone church and runs immediately behind the Culbone Inn. But you can most easily reach it from the pub car park, joining it at the gate standing just a few yards down from where the cars are parked.

This first section of the circular walk is lovely. A wide grassy path, hemmed in by hedges, descends gradually down into a wooded combe. In the distance are the moorland hills of inland Exmoor as they roll towards Simonsbath. Ignore the path leading off to the right, and continue downhill, keeping the combe all the while down to your left.

Gradually the path narrows, but it remains clear and well-trodden.

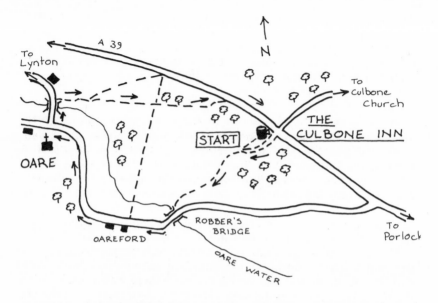

You find yourself walking through heather; there is bracken here, and gorse too: typical moorland vegetation. And all the while the trees below are getting closer.

At the bottom you reach a gate and the path descends suddenly to the road. A little stone bridge stands in front and, to the left (probably) some cars are parked. For this is Robber's Bridge, a popular tourist spot, and one thought to be associated with the Doones in RD Blackmore's famous novel.

Once over the bridge you turn right along the road, keeping the river to your right. Very shortly you come to Oareford, a farmstead sited around an old ford across the river known as Oare Water. This must be a ford of great antiquity, since it once carried a route that ran from the coast to the ancient burial sites on Elsworthy, above the Upper Exe. Today the main route runs east-west and not north-south, so the ford no longer has a function.

From Oareford to Oare church you walk along the country lane, which accompanies the Oare Water down its valley. But what a lovely little lane it is! Narrow and quiet, shaded along its course by tall trees, mostly oak and ash. All around the moorlands tower up above your head, their rolling green slopes interlocking as they disappear into the distance. Gradually, as you continue down the river, the valley widens and the farmland becomes more fertile.

Oare, with its little church and just a couple of other buildings, is an idyllic spot – and justly famous. In *Lorna Doone* it plays a central role – as the home of John Ridd and his neighbour Farmer Snow. It was in Oare church that Lorna was shot by the evil Carver Doone, during the wedding service. Interestingly, inside the church today, can be seen two memorials. One to Blackmore himself, whose grandfather was rector here, and another to a real member of the Snow family.

The journey back to Culbone begins down the lane opposite the church, signposted to Lynmouth and Porlock. This goes down the gentle valley side and crosses the Oare Water by a stone bridge. Immediately on the far side of this bridge, take the footpath off to the right, going through a gate and along the river bank. After a short while you cross a rivulet, flowing down the hillside from your left. Now you bear left yourself, a footpath signpost marking the way. There are in fact two paths here. One heading sharp left, running up the bottom of the combe, and one half-left running steeply up the ridge to the skyline. Take the latter.

This is a very steep climb, up a narrow path across the grass. The frequent stops, to regain your breath, will allow you to look round and admire the views. And as you climb so these views open out. At the top you continue in the same direction (eastwards) along the line of a fence dotted with small trees. The ascent is more gentle now. Beyond a gate and stile the path is well indicated by regular signposts, pointing the way to the A39 road. Across the open moor aim for the right-hand corner of a small coniferous plantation. There you will find a meeting of ways: Yenworthy to the left, Oareford to the right, the A39 straight on. Take the latter – a clear gravel track which leads to a gate and stile. Go straight on along the edge of a field (with hedge on your right) to a distant woodland. There you bend left to join the road. Turn right.

The last stretch is, sadly, along the main road. The distance is about ½ mile. It just seems longer because of the traffic. Still, there is always the hospitality of the Culbone Inn to revive your spirits.

9 Porlock
The Ship Inn

This is not only one of the most famous pubs on Exmoor, but also one of the oldest. It is said to date back to the 13th century. In those days Porlock was still a coastal settlement and its Saxon-built palace was still the centre of a royal hunting chase. In later centuries the Ship became an important coaching inn and a popular venue amongst the local deer hunting fraternity. In the early 19th century it was the favourite haunt of the poets Coleridge and Southey: in 1869 it was mentioned by RD Blackmore in his romantic novel *Lorna Doone*.

The Ship is as picturesque inside as it is outside. Old beams everywhere, stone floors on different levels, comfortable wooden furniture, inglenook corners: all is truly traditional. The walls are hung with seascapes and pictures of old Porlock, doorways lead seemingly in all directions. The place is much bigger inside than it looks from the street: a large main room has the bar area separated at one end, and down some steps is a large restaurant. On the other side of the archway is a games room, to be used on request.

This is a freehouse serving real ales (including Bass and Cotleigh), draught cider and a large selection of wines. But it is the food that brings customers back time and time again. The choice is wondrous to behold, the quality excellent and the prices extremely reasonable. There is an exhaustive regular menu, plus daily specials written up on the blackboards: everything from light snacks to blow-out meals. There are soups, ploughman's lunches, jacket potatoes, open sandwiches, hamburgers, steaks, grills, meat pies, seafood platters and so on. Local venison and pheasant are cooked in season. There is a children's menu and a full range of desserts, whilst vegetarians are offered cheese and vegetable bakes.

The Ship Inn, fortunately, keeps longer than normal pub opening times (10 am to 3 pm and 5.30 pm to 11 pm).

Telephone: 01643 862507.

How to get there: Porlock stands along the A39 road between Minehead (which is 6 miles eastward) and Lynton (10 miles westward). It is now 1 mile from the open sea. The Ship Inn will be found along the southern side of the main road, in Porlock's high street. It is almost opposite the turning that goes down to Porlock Weir and Toll Road that goes round Porlock Hill.

Parking: The Ship does have its own car park – a great advantage in a village with precious few parking places. A public pay car park will be found at the eastern end of Porlock. Vehicles may also be left, freely, well away from the centre, in the housing estates down Villes Lane, where the circular walk begins.

Length of the walk: 4 miles. Map: OS Landranger sheet 181 Minehead and Brendon Hills (inn GR 884467).

There are many walks to be had from Porlock: along the coastal footpath in both directions; down across the meadows to the beach; inland along the wooded valleys to Dunkery Beacon. This walk takes in some of the lovely little villages that nestle below Selworthy Beacon – Bossington, Allerford and West Luccombe. Throughout there are fine views to be had, as the route takes you across meadows and through hillside woodlands. Clear footpaths are used, and well-trodden gravel trackways. Few steep slopes are involved. It is, therefore, a relatively easy walk.

The Walk

Porlock has many old and beautiful buildings, numerous shops selling holiday items, and not a few places of refreshment. You can admire them all on the first leg of your circular walk, since the route leads eastwards from the Ship Inn along the length of the High Street. But dally not for too long. For there is a lovely walk ahead of you.

At the far end of the High Street, just before leaving Porlock, turn left down Villes Lane. This leads past some new housing estates (on

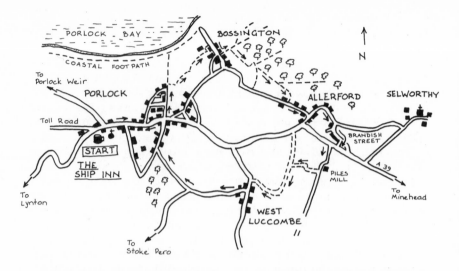

the left-hand side) and ends at a corner with Bay Road. A footpath leads onward, between hedges, and a signpost declares footpaths to Bossington and the beach. The beach-bound path leads across a stile at the first bend in the footpath; the Bossington route keeps to the right, along the double hedge.

The route to Bossington is clearly signposted all the way. At the end of the double hedge a stile leads through to open fields. Keeping to the field edges, and turning left on your way, you aim for the rooftops of Bossington which you can see peeping up over the trees in front. To your left are the Porlock meadows and the sea; ahead is the great green lump which is Selworthy Beacon. A gate takes you back onto a hedge-fringed path, which leads directly to the outlying farms of Bossington. At the gravel track turn left, then right to emerge at the road by Lower House. Now turn right again to reach the main part of the village.

What a pleasant little village Bossington is – old stone cottages, many with thatched roofs, and a timeless charm. Beyond the Old Bakehouse, where teas and other light refreshments are available, turn left along a shady gravel track to a ford and footbridge. The Orchard Guest House should be on your right, the public car park and toilets on your left.

At this spot you stand on the edge of National Trust property. A signpost here points left to Hurlstone and right to Selworthy. Take the latter. This is an attractive path leading right, through a kissing-gate, and onward under the trees, contouring along the wooded hillside. After a while you turn left, climb some steps, follow a field edge up a short way and then turn right, once again to contour along. Down to your right, throughout this section, are views across the Porlock meadows, glimpsed through the trees.

Beyond the next gate, ignore the path leading up to the left signposted to North Hill and Minehead – unless, of course, you intend to lengthen your circuit by climbing Selworthy Beacon. Shortly after this, fork left, ignoring another path leading down to the right. Eventually you come to some houses and a kissing-gate, shortly after which you take the path to the right signposted to Allerford.

This path runs down to a river bank and thence to a footbridge. Across this you reach the road, where you turn left along Allerford village street. Here is another pretty village. The old school is now the West Somerset Rural Life Museum, and all is quiet, old and stone-built. At the top end of the High Street turn left over the ancient packhorse bridge and follow the lane as it climbs and bends right to Higher Allerford. Be sure to stop, and admire the buildings around the packhorse bridge – especially the one with the columned portico. Beyond Higher Allerford bear right down to Brandish Street and left along beside the red sandstone farm buildings that so dominate this hamlet. Here is another pleasant spot, almost in the shadow of Horner Hill, across the valley.

Past the farm buildings turn right to the A39 road which you cross, taking the lane opposite signposted to Piles Mill. After following this lane round, as it passes the mill, take the gravel trackway that leads up to the right. This is opposite the rear of Piles Mill and is signposted to West Luccombe and Horner. It is a clear earth and grass track leading up between hedges, probably the remnants of a once-important route across the valley. In due course, it kinks a bit, descends and is joined by another, similar, track coming up from the right. Continue along, this eventually bringing you out to West Luccombe village. A gate, a footbridge and a nearby ford (for horse traffic) take you to the road where you turn left.

The way back to Porlock leads along the lane signposted to 'Filter Station', a lane which is 'unsuitable for heavy vehicles'. But before turning down here take a closer look at West Luccombe, especially the ancient packhorse bridge. This walk has certainly spoilt you with regards to attractive villages.

The lane back climbs steeply under the trees, bears right and levels off, offering views to the sea on the right. At the fork keep right, walking past the water treatment site and down through the woods. As you approach the outskirts of Porlock the lane gets steeper, and the trees sparser. Eventually you find yourself walking past some curiously gothic, thatched cottages – a fittingly rustic return to the High Street where you turn left to reach the Ship Inn.

Exford
10 The Crown Hotel

The bar entrance, to the left of the main hotel and restaurant entrance, leads through to one main room separated into two by a fine wood and glass screen. Inside, all is cosy, dark and traditional. On the walls are hung old prints, photographs and sporting guns, and the furniture consists of settle benches and wooden tables. Beams cross the ceiling and timber support posts surround the walls. This decor may not, perhaps, be entirely compatible with the age of the building but is very attractive nevertheless.

However, it is the friendly welcome and excellent food that people come here to enjoy. The menu does not give a vast and varied choice and is all the better for it. All the items have been especially planned and are wonderfully presented. There is a distinct flavour of France. Bar snacks include, apart fom the ubiquitous ploughman's lunches and home-made soups, such offerings as pork terrine marinated in wine and port, and grilled tomatoes stuffed with goat's cheese. Main meals include, apart from steaks and fish dishes, such choice delicacies as salmon in soy, ginger and spring onion sauce. Desserts feature chocolate mousse and poached peaches.

The Crown Hotel is a freehouse, its pub section maintaining normal pub opening times. The real ales served include Boddingtons, Flowers Original and Brakspear; the draught cider is Dry Blackthorn. As befits a place serving French-style food there is a wide selection of wines. There are gardens at the rear, popular when the weather is fine.

Telephone: 01643 831554.

How to get there: Exford lies in the heart of Exmoor, 6 miles south of Porlock Bay and below the heights of Dunkery Beacon. Minehead is 10 miles to the north-east; Lynton 11 miles to the north-west. The village lies on the B3224 road about half-way between Wheddon Cross and Simonsbath. The Crown Hotel stands at the junction of that road and the lane running north to Porlock.

Parking: There is a large pub car park. Almost opposite the Crown there is also a free public car park. Parking in the village streets may be difficult, especially during the busy summer months.

Length of the walk: 3 miles. Map: OS Landranger sheet 181 Minehead and Brendon Hills (inn GR 854385).

This is a most beautiful spot. The Upper Exe valley cuts deeply into the moorland landscape, the steep farmlands giving way to heather and bracken as the slopes slacken towards the summits. Patches of woodland line the narrow combes. There are many walks to be had all around: northwards to Wilmersham Common and Dunkery, south-eastwards along the Exe to Winsford, south to the river Barle and Tarr Steps.

This circular walk gives a taste of this scenery. Clear footpaths are used throughout, together with two short stretches of quiet country lane. But some steep slopes are encountered, many stiles and areas of dense undergrowth. So walkers should be prepared.

The Walk

From outside the Crown Hotel, take the B3224 opposite, in the direction signposted to Simonsbath and Lynton. This stretch is called Chapel Street and leads directly to the bridge over the river Exe, where stands (to your right) the White Horse public house.

Exford is a pretty village, sited on an ancient trackway that ran across Exmoor. The Saxons used that route and also, possibly, the Celts before them, since two Iron Age hill forts were sited locally. Today Exford is the home of the Devon and Somerset Stag Hounds and a popular tourist centre.

The footpath that begins the walk will be found to the right of the row of cottages opposite the bridge, the gravel track leading uphill. This soon becomes a wide grassy track as it climbs out of the village between hedges and under trees. At the top is a stile, beyond which

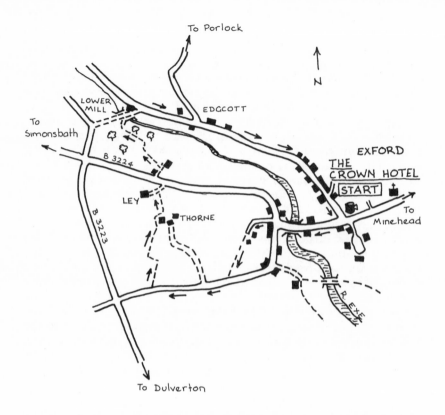

you go straight on, across a farm track and through a wooden gate. Keep the farm and bungalow over to your left. Along by a fence you cross another stile, climb through a clump of trees to a third stile and across the field up to the gate at the top. At the road turn right.

This first stretch has required some climbing, but the views which open out behind should bring their reward. The village now lies below you with the main Exe valley, and numerous side valleys, creating a wonderfully sloping countryside.

The road is only a minor country lane so your walk along it should be pleasant. The views are now to the right, as you continue to gain height. In less than ½ mile the slope slackens and the lane bears slightly left. Ahead you will see the road junction called Chibbet Post, once the site of a gibbet. Readers of RD Blackmore may know this as the place where Red Jem Hannaford was hanged for sheep stealing.

On the right, before Chibbet Post, however, is the stile that leads through to the next section of the circular walk. The path leads up, then down, along the edge of a field (with the hedge to your right) and then through a gate, down the edge of another field (this time with the hedge to your left). Through a gap in the hedge at the bottom corner you turn left, soon followed by a right turn after passing into the next field. You are now walking steeply downhill with the fence to your right. Be sure not to lose your balance looking at the view ahead, and not at your feet. The Exe valley cuts across the scene in the middle distance, the moors of Wilmersham Common can be seen on the distant skyline. Down below is the pretty combe where stands the lonely farmstead called Thorne.

The route in fact leads down to Thorne, around the back of the farm buildings and up the other side of the valley to the hamlet of Ley. Initially the path keeps close to the fence, over the stile, and then round to the right through two gates. It then heads down under the trees, over the stream, across another stile and up across a field. If you aim to the right of the buildings at Ley you should emerge onto the road, close to a private tennis court.

Turn left when you join the road but then almost immediately right, down a gravel track to North Ley Farm. There is a signpost indicating a footpath to Lower Mill. This is the route you want. From the gate next to North Ley Farm head diagonally across the field down to the bottom corner. There a gap in the hedge leads through to a narrow, grassy gulley which takes you round to a gate. The Exe valley can now be seen through the trees to your right, and Lower Mill can be seen below and ahead.

The path down to Lower Mill is steep and clearly marked. But it also runs through deep undergrowth. After wet weather this stretch can be distinctly damp. At the bottom you will find a ford, a footbridge, a gravel track and a delightful little cottage. At the road turn right.

The way back to Exford is now by country lane, through the hamlet of Edgcott. It is a pleasant walk, along the floor of the Exe valley. For much of the distance – beyond Edgcott in fact – you will notice a raised stone pavement, this acting as a dry causeway in times of flood. Upon entering Exford you will see the Crown Hotel on your left.

11 **Dulverton**
The Bridge Inn

This popular, friendly pub is comfortable, unpretentious and spacious: the perfect place to stop. Families are welcome; there is a garden for use in good weather, and the range of food and drink offered is superlative. What more can one say?

There is one large bar room inside, but a screen helps divide this into two sections. The decor is traditional and the walls are hung with pictures of local scenes. The clientele consists of a happy mixture of locals, tourists and walkers, this producing a pleasant buzz of conviviality. The Bridge Inn is a freehouse, opening during normal pub times only.

The real ales sold include John Smith's and Courage Best, the draught cider is Taunton Traditional, and there is a wide selection of house wines. But it is the choice of food offered that makes this pub so well-known. It boasts over 40 items, these being listed in a regular menu and on a blackboard where daily specials are chalked up. There are bar snacks of all kinds, soups, pâtés, jacket potatoes with various fillings, salads, steaks, chicken Kievs and numerous 'pot meals' like chilli con carne. Vegetarian dishes – lasagnes, vegetable bakes and so on – are also provided, and special children's menus. There are desserts and coffee for those with room to spare.

Telephone: 01398 23694.

How to get there: Dulverton stands at the southern edge of Exmoor, in Somerset but very close to the Devon border. It is 10 miles north of Tiverton, and the same distance west of Wiveliscombe. It is most easily reached from the A396 road, that runs along the Exe valley (little more than a mile away eastwards) to which the town is connected by the B3222. The Bridge Inn will be found easily – next to the bridge at Dulverton's southern end.

Parking: There is a pub car park. There are also various public pay car parks around town – for Dulverton is a popular tourist centre. A few free spaces may be found here and there where lay-bys permit.

Length of the walk: 3½ miles. Map: OS Landranger sheet 181 Minehead and Brendon Hills (inn GR 913278).

Dulverton is called the 'Gateway to Exmoor' and it is, indeed, an excellent centre from which the surrounding countryside can be explored. There are walks in all directions. The town stands on the river Barle, close to its confluence with the river Exe. This means that both upland walks, and valley walks, can be enjoyed.

This circular route combines upland and valley scenery, thus giving a splendid introduction to the immediate area. After making a gradual ascent of Court Down the route descends into the Barle valley to follow the river bank back. All the paths used are easy to find, even those that cross farmland.

The Walk

The route begins from the church but, with time permitting, a tour of Dulverton should be made first. It is a pretty little town with many interesting buildings, both literary and historic associations, and a number of friendly shops. There is a weavers' studio, an art exhibition and a National Park Information Centre. There are, in addition, many places selling light refreshments, should the pubs be shut.

Take the narrow tarmac path that leads up the steps along the outside of the church, along its eastern end. That is, keep the church to your left. At the top you come to a lane, where you turn left, to a dead end at the Dulverton primary school. From here you take the footpath off to the right, leading up between hedge banks and under the trees. A lovely little stretch this, and deservedly popular with both locals and tourists. In consequence, it is well-worn.

Ignoring any other tracks leading off to the left, keep to the main path, as it climbs up along the avenue of trees. Now and again a

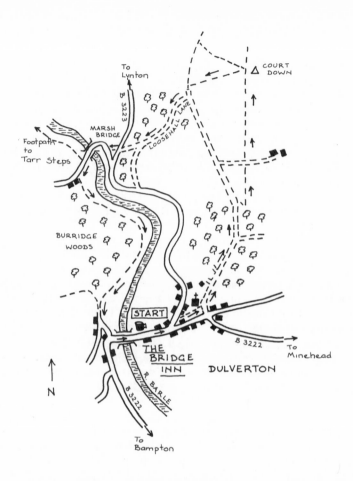

glimpse may be had back to the left, as the view over the Barle valley begins to open out. After a while the path dips a little, levels out and then begins its climb again, all the while leaving Dulverton further behind. A deeply wooded combe can be seen down to the right – an attractive prospect. Shortly the path bends left as another track leads down to the right. Ignore the latter and continue to climb, with the main path. Another wooded combe can now be seen down to the left. What a lovely area this is! This combe to the left is in fact the Barle valley again, along the bottom of which you will be returning to Dulverton later in the walk.

Soon you reach the edge of the trees. The main path leads ever onwards and upwards but here you can leave this popular trackway by turning sharp right (half back) and going through the gate which is set at an angle to the hedgerow. This leads into a field. Turn sharp left, to reach the adjoining field over an earth bank. Now cross diagonally towards the right-hand end of some trees, where you will find a gateway. Along this stretch keep the steep grassy slope, that leads down to a little combe, to your right. Continue along a track to another gate. Northcombe Farm is clearly seen across the valley to the right. Now cross the farm track that runs down to that farm.

The purpose of this diversion from the main, more popular, path, is to reach the top of Court Down directly. The route lies roughly parallel to the main path but further east. From the farm track continue straight on, along the edges of two fields all the while keeping the hedgerow to your left. The climb is gradual. At the top you come out onto the summit of Court Down, the Trig. Point concrete pedestal standing at the centre of an open pasture field. The views now are all around. Winsford Hill can be seen to the north-west, the Brendon Hills to the north-east. Court Down is not very high – just over 1,000 feet – but the panorama is excellent.

The route down begins westwards: from the trig point aim for the left-hand end of a line of small trees growing along a hedgebank. There is a gate in the corner of the field. From there head downhill, keeping the hedge on the left and the wooded slopes of the Barle valley in the distance ahead. Round a small pond to the bottom corner, you turn left through a gate onto an old metalled lane and then, almost immediately, right down a trackway leading down through the trees. This is narrow and dark but very clear, worn down to an earthy, stony surface. It is in fact the top end of an old way called Loosehall Lane, once used by local farmers when taking cattle up to the moors, for summer pasturing.

Follow this trackway all the way down to the main road (the B3223), ignoring another track leading off to the left as you approach the bottom. The route is signposted to Marsh Bridge. Across the road, take the well-worn route cutting off the junction corner and bear left to cross the main bridge over the river Barle. On the far side a sign states that the path continues 250 yards further up on the left. And so it does, through Kennel Farm where a footpath post points the way to Dulverton.

The last stretch, along the river Barle, is very clear, very popular and very beautiful. Ignore any other tracks that may lead off to the right, or gates leading into fields to the left. Follow the main earthy path, stony in parts, that leads through Burridge Woods. Soon the river bubbles along with you to the left, and the occasional rocky crag sticks out to the right. What a lovely end to a splendid walk. At the far end you join a country lane that leads down to the Bridge Inn where refreshment awaits.

Wheddon Cross
The Rest And Be Thankful

Once a coaching inn, and dating from the early 19th century, this pub continues to offer rest and refreshment to weary Exmoor travellers, not just motorists but cyclists and walkers. For Wheddon Cross – the highest village on Exmoor – is something of a focal point for people wishing to enjoy the views and wildlife of this part of Somerset. Dunkery Beacon is little more than 2 miles away.

Inside there are three main bar rooms, the middle one having ceiling beams hung with a vast collection of jugs. The lounge is to one side, the public bar to the other. Behind the latter is a large skittle alley. There is also a separate restaurant. Throughout, the decor is plush but traditional, and there are numerous prints and old photographs decorating the walls, these showing local scenes. The Rest and Be Thankful, which is a freehouse, is a well-known hotel offering luxury accommodation and facilities for private functions. Children are very welcome – the Buttery Bar is especially geared to families – and the patio outside has views across the moors. All in all, this is the most pleasant of places to stop: it is certainly aptly named.

There is a wide choice of real ale, including Ushers, Ruddles and Old Speckled Hen, draught cider and wines. The food ranges from simple bar snacks, like sandwiches, ploughman's lunches, pies and sausages, to gourmet dishes for the discerning palate. There are several Italian dishes on the restaurant menu, and various cheese-based house specials. The evening meals are very popular indeed.

Telephone: 01643 841222.

How to get there: Wheddon Cross, as the name suggests, stands on a crossroads. The A396 Dunster to Tiverton road crosses the B3224 road, that runs from Exford to Bishops Lydeard. Both Porlock and Minehead are 6 miles away, north-westwards and north-eastwards respectively. The Rest and Be Thankful can hardly be missed: it stands at the north corner of the crossroads.

Parking: The large car park immediately behind the pub is used by customers and general public alike. Public conveniences have been built in one corner and the village playing field is close by.

Length of the walk: 4 miles. Map: OS Landranger sheet 181 Minehead and Brendon Hills (inn GR 924388).

Many walkers climb Dunkery Beacon from Wheddon Cross, using well-signposted lanes and bridleways via Dunkery Gate. Dunkery Beacon is the highest point on Exmoor. It rises to over 1,700 feet and offers wonderful views all around. The round trip from Wheddon Cross would be about 6 miles. This walk however is rather shorter, and takes in some of the valleys that surround Wheddon Cross. These are extremely pretty, especially that of the river Avill, along its upper course. Here the Blagdon Woods cover the valley sides affording shelter to a host of wildlife. The route is clear throughout since well-worn bridleways are used almost exclusively. There are some steep slopes, however, and some stretches can be a trifle muddy owing to the churning of the ground by horses' hooves.

The Walk

The route begins at the far corner of the car park behind the Rest and Be Thankful Inn. Next to the public conveniences there is a footpath signpost, pointing to Luckwell Bridge, and the way leads across the village cricket pitch. Should a match be in progress keep to the outside of the boundary rope, or you might find yourself being an unconscious fielder!

A gate to the right of the pavilion leads to a path that runs down the edge of a field. Keeping the hedgerow close to your right you reach another gate, in a deep grassy cleft. Continue through this downhill. By this time the path is running along the bottom of a shallow, grassy gully with a high hedgebank to the right. Down in the valley a gate takes you into an open field, and you leave the trees behind. Keep to

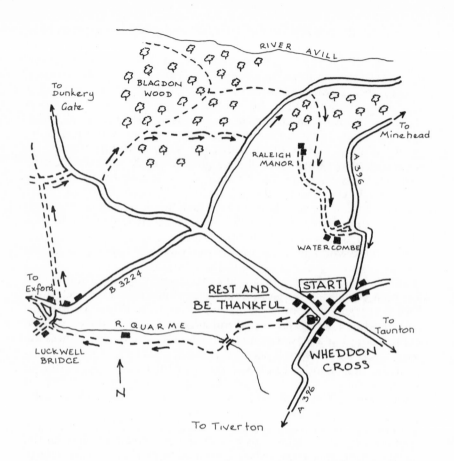

the edge of this field as you cross to a stile which is set into the hedge on your left. This takes you to a footbridge across the stream, on the far side of which turn right, to ascend the field. The stream is now parallel, but some way below you to the right. The gate at the top takes you through to a clear track, running attractively beneath the trees. In due course you pass a little cottage on your right, either side of which a gate crosses the track, to enclose that cottage's garden. Continue on, across the meadow to Luckwell Bridge where the old chapel has been converted into a house. At that point turn right to walk up to the road.

Since Wheddon Cross you have been walking westward, first down into, and then along, the valley of the river Quarme. This is one of the tributaries of the river Exe, rising at the foot of Dunkery Beacon and flowing down to Exton. It is a very attractive river with an unspoilt valley. At this point in the circular walk, however, you head northward, to rise out of the valley towards Dunkery itself.

Keeping to the right as you approach the main road, cross over and take the narrow tarmac lane opposite. This rises steeply between houses, the one on the left being called 'Bull's Eye'. A sign states that this route is 'unsuitable for motors'. Indeed it is, for it soon degenerates into a rutted, gravel track. It is also deeply set in below the high hedgebanks on either side – a hollowed route indicating great antiquity. Follow this track all the way to the top, where you meet a narrow tarmac lane. Turn right, downhill, to meet the lane from Dunkery Gate. Here you continue to the right, downhill.

The bridleway back to Wheddon Cross begins at the point where the tarmac lane bends right. On the left, here, is a bridleway sign pointing through a gate, indicating the way to Blagdon Wood. This clear grassy trackway leads downhill between hedges and through a gate into the woodland. And what a lovely stretch this next section is! Deciduous trees and ferns and, to the left, glimpses of a view across the valley of Bin Combe. In spring and summer there are wild flowers all about, in autumn the glorious golden colours dazzle the eye. At the fork keep right to contour along the valley side. In due course this path reaches a gate at the woodland edge, curves around a little side combe along a grassy slope and then continues eventually to meet the road. Turn left, downhill, along this road.

At the next bend a bridleway goes off to the left, signposted to Dunkery Gate. Opposite – on the right – another bridleway is signposted to Wheddon Cross. Take this latter route – a clear earthy track that climbs slightly as it curves up below the trees. After passing a house up to the right (which is called Raleigh Manor) the track continues to curve right – to reach a gate. Thereafter you meet the metalled lane that comes down from Raleigh Manor. Turn left to follow this lane down to Watercombe. Beyond the farm is the main road where a right turn soon brings you back up to Wheddon Cross.

13 **Wootton Courtenay**
Dunkery Beacon Hotel

What a splendid position this building occupies! Set in its own grounds the hotel commands an elevated site, high above the headwaters of the river Avill. From the lawns and terrace – and indeed, from the windows of the lounge – the sweep of Exmoor can be seen rising towards the National Park's highest point. The summit that dominates the view is in fact Dunkery Hill, not Dunkery Beacon. That is just out of sight, beyond.

For walkers and motorists alike the Dunkery Beacon Hotel provides a perfect stopping place. It is spacious, comfortable and friendly. It also provides a good range of food and drink. It is a freehouse, serving Webster's and Exmoor real ales and a wide choice of wines. The menu books, which list bar snacks and main meals, are not exhaustive in their options. But what the food lacks in variety it gains in quality. There are open sandwiches, jacket potatoes (with various fillings), numerous things with chips, fish dishes and grills. Children have their own menu and vegetarians are catered for – perhaps with vegetable bakes. Portions are generous and everything is home-cooked.

The front entrance leads into the main bar room, with tiled floor, dartboard and skittles. To the left is a very large, and much more plush, lounge with carpets and cushioned seats. The hotel end lies beyond. Those staying at the Dunkery Beacon Hotel are certainly spoilt.

The pub end keeps normal pub opening times. At certain times of year theme weekends are held and special interest groups often stay here for activity holidays.

Telephone: 01643 841241.

How to get there: Wootton Courtenay appears remote, surrounded as it is by hills and moorlands. Yet it is only 4 miles south-east of Porlock and 3 miles south-west of Minehead. It is most easily reached from the A396 Dunster to Wheddon Cross road, taking the turning from Timberscombe. The Dunkery Beacon Hotel stands at the western edge of the village.

Parking: The hotel has its own car park, in its own grounds. Vehicles can also be left, in certain places in the village provided no obstruction is caused.

Length of the walk: 4 miles. Map: OS Landranger sheet 181 Minehead and Brendon Hills (inn GR 936435).

The walk to the top of Dunkery Beacon is very popular – this being a 7 mile round trip. However, those wishing to do a slightly shorter circuit may prefer the route suggested here. This will give a taste of the scenery to be enjoyed by the more energetic. It goes half-way to the Beacon, skirting the base of Dunkery Hill. Moorland paths are used, together with clear farm tracks. Bracken and heather clad slopes are traversed and a little wooded combe is crossed. The route throughout is very clear.

Whilst no great height is achieved – about 1,000 feet compared with the Beacon's 1,704 feet – some glorious views are to be had. The Bristol Channel can be seen, and the coastline of north Somerset towards Weston-super-Mare. If lucky, you may also see some deer.

The Walk

Follow the road eastwards to the village centre and turn right opposite the church. Those interested, should look around this church before proceeding – for it is a splendid example of Gothic architecture. It dates, mostly, from the 13th century but contains some Perpendicular (15th century) stone carvings. Inside, the wagon roofs of the nave and north aisle should be seen.

Down in the valley you continue along the road that runs through the southern end of Wootton Courtenay, across the stream and up out of the village. Just beyond the last house on the right (an attractive, thatched, building) turn right up a narrow tarmac lane signposted as

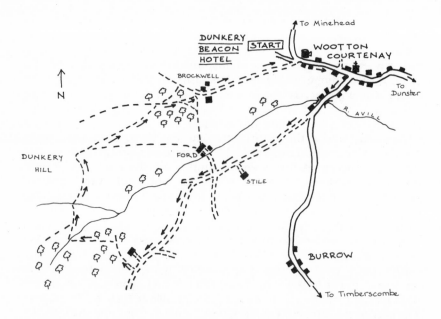

a dead end. This takes you on a long climb out of the valley, eventually levelling to offer views all round. In due course you pass the drive to a place called 'Stile', on the left-hand side. Soon after this two grassy trackways join the lane from the right. The first leads down and half-back, and is a bridleway to 'Ford'. The second leads up, half-right and is a bridleway to 'Span Gate'. Take the latter. Leaving the tarmac behind you now walk along an earthy trackway, that runs darkly beneath the trees with high hedgebanks on either side. Locally this is known as Digland Lane. Keep left at the fork and continue to climb under the spreading branches. After curving right this pleasant track joins a more important, gravel-made trackway. Continue in the same direction along this.

Very shortly, a drive off to the right leads to a large detached house. Immediately beyond, also on the right, a gate leads to a grassy path running through a little woodland. Take this and continue, through another gate, down towards the valley. The dome of Dunkery Hill, round and green, now stands ahead. Keeping left at the fork, this path (in fact, a bridleway) proceeds to contour along the valley side. Beyond the end of the woodland you can see across to the right. Wootton Courtenay lies in the distant valley, with the wooded Grabbist Hill beyond. This is a lovely stretch, with bracken either side and the wild moorland all around and above.

Further on you dip down through some more trees, cross the stream using the boulders as stepping stones, and turn right to follow the path out of the valley. The way through the bracken here is clear. As the path levels a footpath signpost indicates another path, left, to Span Gate. Ignore this and continue in the direction of Brockwell. Soon you cross a side combe, using boulders again to cross the stream, and climb at an angle across the moorland slope. The summit of Dunkery Hill is up to your left. This is wild Exmoor indeed: listen and look for the native deer. You might just be lucky.

Towards the top the path swings left and then, soon after, turns right in order to avoid the farmlands which stretch up to this area from the valleys below. A fork soon presents itself: the track to the right (that keeps close to the wall that divides moorland from farmland) should be ignored. Instead, keep left, to follow the way signposted to 'Iron Pits'. The views from this hillside are splendid indeed. Eastwards along the Avill valley, beyond Dunster, is the Bristol Channel. On a clear day the coast of north Somerset can be seen stretching towards Weston-super-Mare.

The path now crosses the heather, gorse and bracken-clad moorland towards Wootton Courtenay, which you can see in the distance. Just before the trees is a junction. Turn right to Brockwell. The way to the left is to Dunkery Beacon itself. Continue through the woods, keeping right at the first fork and left at the second. A last, steep, descent brings you down to the road by way of an attractive woodland path. Once on the tarmac follow the direction signposted to Wootton Courtenay, passing a thatched house. This narrow lane leads all the way to the village, where it emerges almost opposite the Dunkery Beacon Hotel.

Good walk - lovely valley views but some tough uphill walking.

14 Luxborough
The Royal Oak

Walking into this pub, it is said, is like stepping back 300 years. The floors are laid with Somerset slate flagstones and cobbles, the low ceilings are beamed, the old farmhouse furniture is worn and rustic and the cobwebs are genuine. The place is truly unique and should on no account, be missed.

The building is thought to date back to the 14th century. What is now the front bar – the oldest part – was a cottage, and the dining area, up a step to one side, was a Tudor extension incorporating a hay loft. The back room (the 'Brewhouse Bar') was once a slaughterhouse, the meat being sold at the front, which acted as a butcher's shop. The window from that shop now encloses the bar counter. At a later date the back room was used for making beer – hence its present name. Above that room was a 'pavilion' or games room used by the villagers. This is now private accommodation.

The Royal Oak – known locally and mysteriously as 'The Blazing Stump' – is a freehouse selling any number of real ales, from regulars like Cotleigh Tawny and Flowers IPA, to several local and lesser known brews, Exmoor Gold for instance. And the food is superb, from normal bar fare items to daily specials written up on the blackboards. There are salads, jacket potatoes, various fish dishes, wholesome meat and ale pies and so on. Rabbit stew may feature, pigeon breasts or the intriguing 'carpet bag chicken'. Not for nothing is this pub widely popular. The Royal Oak, which maintains normal pub opening times, also offers accommodation. There is a garden at the back, and all are welcome.

Telephone: 01984 40319.

How to get there: Luxborough is a small village almost lost amidst the hills of Exmoor, in that area more commonly known as the Brendon Hills. It is just 6 miles south of Minehead. It can be reached from the B3224 road, from near its junction with the A396 at Wheddon Cross. It may also be reached from Timberscombe, which is west of Dunster. The Royal Oak will be found at Kingsbridge, ½ mile east of Churchtown – for Luxborough is in two separate parts.

Parking: There is a car park immediately behind the Royal Oak, reserved for customers. Opposite, and round the corner, is a large public car park – a gravelled area of field with an honesty box. Elsewhere in the village parking space is limited by the narrowness of the lanes.

Length of the walk: 3 ½ miles. Map: OS Landranger sheet 181 Minehead and Brendon Hills (inn GR 984377).

Luxborough is an idyllic little village in an idyllic location. There are lanes, bridleways and footpaths spreading out in all directions and every one of these offers splendid walking opportunities. Valley walks provide woodland scenery, fast streams and lowland wildlife; hill walks give views far across the Brendon Hills. This route – almost entirely along bridleways – includes both upland ridges and deep, wooded combes. It thus covers all that a walker could wish for – and in just a relatively short distance. However, there are some steep slopes to negotiate, so the correct footwear should be worn.

The Walk

Outside the Royal Oak walk downhill, over the bridge that crosses the little Washford river and right along the lane signposted to Wheddon Cross. Then, almost immediately, bear left to walk up the track that runs past the village hall. The village car park – the gravelled corner of a field – is opposite. There is a bridleway sign here pointing to Lower Court Farm and Treborough.

The way to Lower Court Farm is easy to follow for there are regular bridleway markings and the track is well-used. This track at first is tarmac, since it leads to a cottage, but soon changes to one of grass and

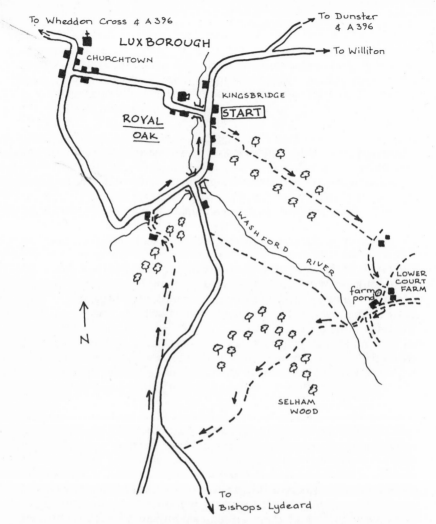

stones. It is fairly steep with a tall hedgerow on either side. When you stop to regain your breath make sure you look behind, for the view northwards across Luxborough soon opens out as you gain height. Towards the top of the slope the track narrows as it approaches a pedestrian/horse gate (as opposed to a normal size farm gate). Beyond this you continue in the same direction until further gates (of usual size) lead through to an open field. The way now continues along a ridge and the views on either side are superb. Keeping the fence and hedge to your left you soon reach a stile and gate, in front of some barns. Keeping these buildings to your left bear right along a gravel track that curves, through a gate, to reach Lower Court Farm down in the valley. Turn right after the next gate and walk through the farmyard (past the farm pond) to the tarmac lane at the end. Turn right again and go downhill past the farmhouse and another cottage. Ignore the track that leads off to the left and continue down to the valley bottom where you cross a rivulet, as it bubbles across the field.

This is the same valley in which Luxborough stands, but further upstream. It is a beautiful spot and seemingly undisturbed by the modern world. You may wish to linger here, and soak up the atmosphere.

Having stepped over the rivulet turn right to follow the watercourse into the next field. Those wishing to shorten the walk may care to continue down the path that leads ahead, along the bottom of the valley. This will take them to the road above Luxborough where they can turn right to reach the Royal Oak. Those wishing to continue the circuit as planned should strike up to the left. This steep climb will bring them to the woodland that runs along the top of the valley side. This is Selham Wood, an attractive area of beech and oak, many of which have been coppiced to produce multi-trunked trees.

Ascending at an angle a gate leads to a path through the trees. This winds up to the top edge of the woodland, where you continue in the same direction to a gate at the top (and far side) of the field, set into the hedgerow on the skyline. Beyond this you continue through another gate and then follow a track that runs up to the left, along by a hedge. The view is now down to the right, across Luxborough. The gate at the top takes you through into a large field that undulates around a shallow combe. Follow the edge of this field round, curving right, keeping the hedgerow all the while to your left. This takes you down, then up, to a gate and the road. Turn right, to walk down the road along which you are soon joined by another road, coming down from the left. Continue further down to a point where the road bends right. From here the return to Luxborough is very straightforward.

A bridleway sign points the way, straight on as the road bends right. Continue along this direction through a number of fields and through a number of gates. All the while keep to the edge of the fields, with the hedgerow on your left. Gradually this route curves left as it reaches the bottom of the valley. At one point you walk through a little wood, but the path is very clear, if a little churned by horses' hooves. Eventually you emerge onto a gravel track, where there is a cottage on the left. Follow this round to the right (not sharp right, where a grassy track leads down by the stream) to reach the road. Now turn right along the road, to walk down to meet a quiet little road junction. Keep left and follow the road that runs along the valley floor back to the Royal Oak.

⑮ Dunster
The Foresters Arms

Inside all is mock-Tudor, with cottage-style wooden furniture, brick pillars and timber-panelled walls. The bar counter is topped by a mini, tiled roof. However, the friendliness and welcome are real enough for this is a cosy pub despite its great size. The main bar room is very large but is pleasantly sub-divided into separate areas – a public bar with dartboard and pool table, a lounge, a dining area and, beyond, a family room. There is also a restaurant. Elsewhere are other facilities for the Foresters Arms also offers accommodation.

It is a freehouse selling such real ales as Boddingtons and Marston's Pedigree. Draught ciders and various wines are also offered. But it is the food here that draws people to this end of Dunster (away from the busier, more touristy end). The menus, both for the bar snacks and the main meals, are extensive and very reasonably priced. All manner of items are prepared, from soups, salads, burgers and ploughman's lunches to things with chips, gammon, chicken, steak and fish dishes. Vegetarians are not forgotten and children have their own menu. Normal pub opening times are kept, but with some latitude.

Telephone: 01643 821313.

How to get there: Dunster is a well-known tourist honeypot, and understandably so since it is a most attractive, ancient and historic town. Dunster Castle towers above the houses in the main street. In consequence, the place is not difficult to find – just 2 miles down the road from Minehead. It is situated where the A39 road to Williton is joined by the A396 from Wheddon Cross. The Foresters Arms stands at the southern end.

Parking: The pub does not have its own car park adjoining but there is a car park at the bottom of the road that runs down from the Foresters Arms to Gallox Bridge. There is also a large public car park at the other end of Dunster, near the junction with the A39. Dunster gets very busy in the summer and parking spaces are naturally restricted. Park at the edge and walk in to the town centre.

Length of the walk: 4 miles. Map: OS Landranger sheet 181 Minehead and Brendon Hills (inn GR 989434).

Dunster alone could provide a walk long enough to raise a thirst: its High Street with the old Yarn Market, its water mill, the medieval packhorse bridge, the folly-topped Conygar Hill overlooking the town at its northern end, and the castle, which dominates Dunster's southern end. This walk, however, stretches beyond the town's boundaries, to the wooded slopes all around.

From Grabbist Hill superb views can be enjoyed, across Minehead and the sea towards Wales; from Vinegar Hill the Avill valley can be appreciated. Walkers should be prepared for some steep slopes. However, those wishing to shorten the route will be able to do so.

The Walk

Outside the Foresters Arms turn right along the main road, in the direction of Dunster town centre. Before the church, however – that is, before the traffic lights that control vehicle flow through the town centre – turn left. This road is called St George's Street and is opposite the entrance to Dunster Castle. Continue up this road, past Priory Green on the right and the school on the left. Although you want the path to Grabbist Hill, you can ignore the sign you first meet, just past the school. This leads to a path that takes a slightly longer route to the summit. You could take it, of course, but it might be wiser to take the next path you come to. This will be found a little further on, starting from the corner of Hangers Way. This is a dark, tree-shaded path called Conduit Lane, a gravel track that – as the name might suggest – can be wet in damp weather. Between hedges this leads up to a gate, beyond which you turn left, to follow a much drier

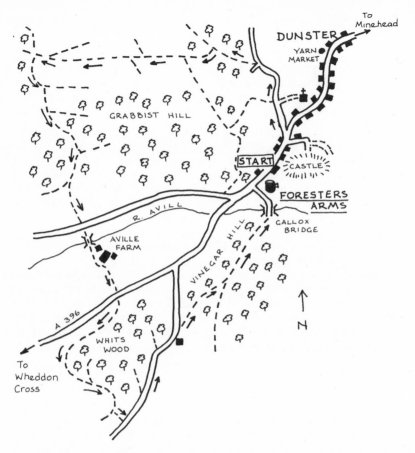

track that curves uphill. Do not take the pathway that leads straight on from the gate, unless of course, you wish to walk to Minehead.

The long steady climb to the top of Grabbist Hill need not be described in detail. Ignore other paths coming in from the left or going off to the right. Continue straight on and up. Here and there a wooden bench has been thoughtfully positioned – to offer rest and allow you to appreciate the ever-widening views. And what views they are. At first to the right only, across Minehead and the Bristol Channel towards Wales, but later (as the path levels off and you emerge from the trees) to the left also, across the Avill valley to Croydon Hill and the Brendons. No wonder the National Trust is pleased to own this end of Grabbist Hill – you pass its notice on the way up. All around is heather and bracken and – further away – are the dark green plantations.

As you approach the trees at the top a track joins from the right. Soon after, at the edge of the plantation, there is a meeting of ways. The gate ahead leads to a plantation track. The track to the half-right is signposted to Selworthy. The track to the left leads to Croydon Hill, and this is the one to follow. After a short distance only, this track bends left and leaves the trees behind. Now turn right down another gravel track. This goes very steeply downhill. At the bottom of the steepest section turn half-left, along a narrower track that runs between the trees. Do not turn sharp left, along the larger track, for this is a plantation track only.

Once again, you now descend steeply, eventually reaching a main track that you follow round to the right. After just a few yards turn left, down a path through the bracken that leads to a tarmac lane. Go straight over, cross a footbridge, and continue, past Aville Farm, to the main road. Incidentally, those now wishing to shorten their walk can turn left, either along the tarmac lane or along the main road. This will take them back to Dunster.

Across the main road, and through a gate, a footpath leads uphill along the edge of a field. Keeping the hedgerow to your right aim for the woodland on the skyline. At the top corner a track continues, now through the woodland itself. This track – which offers an excellent walk through Whits Wood – scribes a long curve to the left, all the while keeping the steep, tree-covered slope up to the left. At the far end, bear left through a Forestry Commission bar-gate to reach the road. Turn left to walk downhill past the Nutcombe Bottom car park. Soon after this the road bends left, as it passes a cottage.

The last section, back to the Foresters Arms, offers a beautiful walk through woods, around Vinegar Hill. The track contours so no steep climbing is involved, and the views through the trees to the left are lovely. For most of the way there are rhododendrons either side, so in springtime the colours also are splendid. This track leaves the road, on the right-hand side, just after the bend and cottage. It reaches Dunster at Gallox Bridge, the medieval packhorse bridge at the bottom of Park Street. What an excellent end to the walk! The Foresters Arms stands at the top end of Park Street, along which there are some old, thatched cottages. Not far is the 17th century water mill, and this should be seen if time permits.

Watchet
The Clipper Inn

There may be plusher pubs in town, and more trendy pubs, but few could be friendlier than this. The Clipper Inn also has the advantage of being open all afternoon every day except Sunday – the opening times being noon to 11 pm.

Once known as the London Inn, this has old-world charm without being pretentious. There is timber framing on the bar-room walls, and the furniture is rustic but nothing has been especially planned or designed to meet present day 'style' fashions. Everything is cosy and welcoming, homely and comfortable. No wonder the place is very popular.

There are three small rooms: a public bar on the left as you enter, a lounge on the right and, beyond the latter, a separate dining room. The dining room is the quietest of the three, and the one favoured by families. This is pleasantly furnished in the style of a private house. In winter months an open fire burns and the place becomes particularly cheery.

As a Courage house the Clipper Inn serves Directors and Courage Best real ales, together with Taunton Traditional and Dry Blackthorn cider. Various wines are also available. Good wholesome food is provided, from snacks like sandwiches and burgers to main meals like chicken, fish dishes and lasagne. Everything is very reasonably priced and well presented. So there should be nothing to stop you enjoying your visit here – unless, of course, you happen to be superstitious. For there is a resident ghost!

Telephone: 01984 631880.

How to get there: Watchet is a small harbour town just 7 miles east of Minehead. It stands close to where the Doniford Stream flows into the Bristol Channel. It is the Doniford valley that separates the Quantocks from the Brendon Hills – so both these attractive areas are within easy reach. The town is approached from the A39 road which runs through Williton. The Clipper Inn backs onto the West Pier of the harbour.

Parking: There is no pub car park here but a large public car park will be found close by. In fact, Watchet has several large public car parks, of the 'pay and display' variety. Parking elsewhere may be difficult – especially during summer months.

Length of the walk: 2½ miles. Map: OS Landranger sheet 181 Minehead and Brendon Hills (inn GR 071435).

Watchet is a pretty little town notwithstanding its industries in general and its paper mill in particular, that so dominate the landward side. There are many old buildings and a pleasant time can be had strolling around the narrow streets. The harbour has an attractive esplanade and the boats offer an interesting backdrop. This little walk, out of town, will be especially enjoyed by those interested in steam trains. It follows an old mineral line route that runs beside a section of the West Somerset Railway, a popular local tourist attraction. The hilltop St Decuman's church is also visited – from where there are views over the town. The way is clear throughout and can be enjoyed by almost everybody.

The Walk

The circuit begins almost opposite the Clipper Inn. Turn right outside the front entrance, cross the stream, and turn left down Mill Lane. There is a footpath sign here, pointing the way down the Old Mineral Line. Walk past the 'Star at Watchet' pub, round by the Royal British Legion Club and then bear right to follow a residential street called 'Whitehall'. At the far end of this keep to the right, taking the tarmac track signposted 'No Unauthorised Motor Vehicles. Public Footpath only'. Beyond the last of the buildings another footpath leads off to the right (to Blue Anchor Road) but you keep straight on in the direction of Washford. This wide tarmac path becomes gravel-surfaced after going under the railway bridge but it is clear and firm

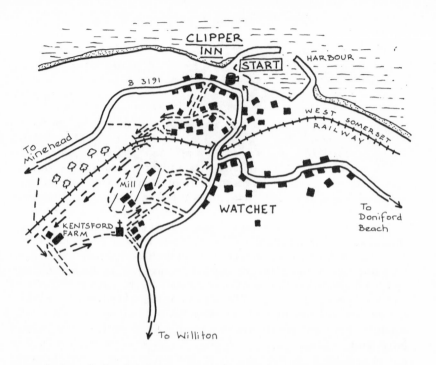

nonetheless. Indeed, it is an extremely popular route, and all the way to Washford it is used by locals, tourists and dog owners. Along this stretch it is also accompanied, to the right, by the West Somerset Railway and steam trains frequently pass by, especially during the summer months.

This Watchet to Washford track follows the line of the old West Somerset Mineral Railway. In the second half of the 19th century iron ore extraction in the Brendon Hills grew into a major local industry. This rail connection was built to bring the ore from the mines and quarries at Goosemoor (east of Wheddon Cross) to Watchet, from where it could be shipped to South Wales. The route included a spectacular incline, that took the line down to the upper Washford valley, whence it followed the stream through the villages of Roadwater and Torre. But this industry did not last long. By the 1880s it was in decline and, by the turn of the century, the mineral line had been abandoned.

Across the large paper mill, to the left of the footpath, you can see the tower of St Decuman's church on the top of the hill. It can be seen from all around this district and one can easily imagine how, in years gone by, it acted as a useful landmark to sailors out to sea. Once you leave the mill behind, and reach the open country, the gravel surface underfoot becomes more grassy and earthy. Here and there bench seats have been positioned alongside, so those who wish can take a breather.

In due course you reach a meeting of ways. To the right a footpath leads over a level crossing towards Blue Anchor. To the left another footpath leads through a gate and over a stream towards St Decuman's church. Take the latter – unless, of course, you intend walking all the way to Washford along the old mineral line. Beyond Kentsford Farm (past the old farmhouse with its mullioned windows and arched doorway) climb the stile on the left and cross the field upwards, keeping to the path as it curves to the right. Diagonally across the next field you come to a track that climbs up to the church. Half-way up you may like to see St Decuman's Holy Well down some stone steps to the left, reached through a gate. This is a little spring, now surrounded by stone slabs.

St Decuman was a Welsh missionary who founded this holy site, so it is said, after crossing the Bristol Channel on a raft. He built a cell here and lived almost hermit-like, supplied only by the waters of his well and food generously offered by locals. He was murdered by a Dane, during one of the many raids that Watchet suffered at the hands of the Vikings, but his good works continued to inspire the Saxon inhabitants.

The way back to Watchet begins down the tarmac path that runs from the church, beside a high stone wall. It is labelled as a footpath only and runs past an old mill chimney. There are glimpses of the sea ahead. The route is fairly straight. It crosses a road that leads to the paper mill and goes through a tunnel under the railway line. Turn left when you reach the road.

Now you can wander around town at your leisure. Visit the interesting little museum, sit by the harbour and recall that it was Watchet that inspired Coleridge to write his famous poem *The Ancient Mariner*.

17 Stogumber
The White Horse Inn

This is an excellent example of a village pub – cosy, old-fashioned and friendly. The building is not especially ancient but the furniture is suitably rustic, with bench seats, settles, captain's chairs and plain wooden tables. There is one main bar room but there is another room, at the rear, which has a dartboard and fruit machines. Outside, at the back, is a garden-cum-courtyard. A family room is made available in summer months.

This is a freehouse that keeps normal pub opening times. Local real ales are served – Cotleigh and Exmoor – and, often, Sheppy's draught cider. There is a full selection of wines as well. But it is the food that makes the White Horse unmissable. It is exceptional both in quality and value-for-money. Bar snacks include burgers, bacon rolls and various sandwiches; there are starters like salmon mousse, grills with steak and gammon, fish dishes of trout, seafood and scampi; there are various salads. Some of the main meals are especially mouth-watering – Somerset pork in cider for instance, and 'fish in a poke' which is white fish wrapped in a pastry case. For non-meat eaters there are vegetable pasties and omelettes. Should you still be hungry there are many sweets to choose from – walnut tarts, steamed sultana sponges and numerous ice-cream concoctions. Teas and coffees are also served.

Telephone: 01984 56277.

How to get there: Stogumber is situated at the eastern edge of Exmoor. The Quantock Hills are close at hand whilst the Doniford Stream flows less than a mile away, on its way to Watchet. The village does not stand on a main road but can easily be reached from the A358 Williton to Taunton road. Williton itself is only 3 miles away to the north. The White Horse will be found at the northern end of Stogumber, opposite the church.

Parking: There is a pub car park. Vehicles may also be left opposite, in the space provided close to the churchyard wall. A few other parking places may be found in the village but drivers should be warned that the village streets are narrow and winding.

Length of the walk: 3½ miles. Map: OS Landranger sheet 181 Minehead and Brendon Hills (inn GR 098374).

This walk is to Monksilver and back. Country lanes are used and footpaths across farmland. Here and there the route is not especially clear but the ground underfoot is generally firm and there should be no difficulties in pathfinding – there are no steep slopes or swamps to negotiate.

This is a lovely, unspoilt area with hills, valleys and woods. The views are westwards to the Brendon Hills, and eastwards to the Quantocks. Stogumber itself, and Monksilver, are attractive villages and these should be explored at a leisurely pace.

The Walk

The walk begins down to the right, outside the White Horse, and then right again at the junction, in the direction of Bicknoller and Williton. After 50 yards turn left down the gravel track called The Orchard and then follow the path that descends beside the cottage called Orchard End. This path turns right, to skirt a garden, and then left (beyond a stile) to climb up a field away from the village. But it would be a shame to follow all these directions before looking around Stogumber first. It is one of the prettiest villages in west Somerset.

The medieval church, the colour-washed thatched cottages, the 17th century almshouses, the cobbled lanes: such an ensemble should prove irresistible to lovers of the English countryside and landscape. Stogumber also has historic connections. Much of the church interior was beautified by Cardinal Beaufort, one of the judges on duty at the trials of Joan of Arc, and there are monuments to the Sydenham

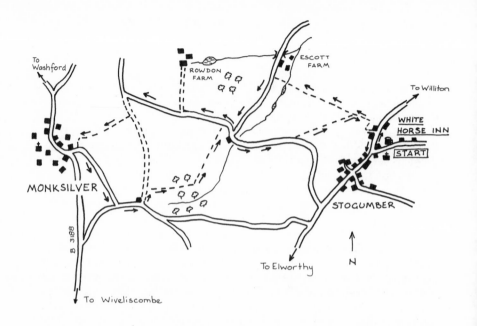

To Washford

ROWDON FARM

ESCOTT FARM

To Williton

WHITE HORSE INN

START

MONKSILVER

B 3188

STOGUMBER

To Elworthy

N

To Wiveliscombe

family, one of whose number, Elizabeth married Sir Francis Drake.

From the first stile you follow a fence up along the edge of one field to a second stile. From here you cross the next field diagonally to a gate, making sure that you appreciate the views on your way across. The Quantocks rise from the Doniford valley over to your right, the Brendon Hills emerge on the skyline ahead. You will be able to enjoy this view later, for you will be returning this way at the end of your walk.

From the gate, the right of way continues in the same direction (north-westwards). Depending upon the nature of the fields at the time of your visit, you can either bear right to a further gate and then left, to follow a hedgerow down to the valley, or else you can go through the near gate and follow the same hedgerow down, but on its other side. Whether the hedgerow is to your right or left you will soon find yourself at the valley floor, with Escott Farm over to your right about 300 yards away. There is a small lake up to your left where the stream has been dammed. Crossing this stream you reach a gate in the top hedgerow, this leading onto the road. Turn left.

You now keep to the tarmac for a while. Follow it up the valley to a junction where stands a large, detached house with a thatched roof. Turn right and keep to the road as it climbs steeply uphill. This is an attractive stretch. The road is quiet and the views to the right are towards Williton. Across the valley is Rowdon Farm and its lake – a pleasant if artificial addition to the scenery. Beyond the drive that leads down to Rowdon the road bends right. At this point turn left, taking a grassy track that runs between high-banked hedgerows. This is known locally as Combecross Lane. After about 200 yards along this track however, turn right and climb a stile that you will see high up in the hedgerow. The way to Monksilver is now straightforward. You follow the edges of several fields keeping the hedgerow all the way on your left. Down at the road turn left to continue the circular walk, bear right to see the village of Monksilver.

This is another beautiful village and time should be set aside for a tour of its lanes. The 15th century church has a Norman tower and contains some excellent examples of medieval woodcarving. The Notley Arms is a popular local hostelry and will satisfy those in need of refreshment.

The way back begins along the lane that climbs steeply out of the valley past the modern-designed Elworthy, Monksilver and Nettlecombe Cummunity Hall. At the top, keep left at the junction to follow the Stogumber direction. Soon you reach a thatched cottage and the lane bears right. At this point turn left immediately beyond the cottage, along a gravel track signposted to Sampford Brett. This happens to be the bottom end of Combecross Lane, that you followed earlier along its top end. Once again, however, you do not follow it for long. Just before a large metal barn there are two farm gates on the right. Go through the second and follow the field edge keeping the hedgerow to your right. At the far end a gate, a short stretch of grassy track and another gate lead you through a narrow belt of trees to another field. Continue along the top edge, with the hedge to your left and the valley down to your right. Along here you descend to the road where you turn right.

This short stretch you may recognise, for you walked up this lane earlier. This time, however, you walk down to the junction and continue straight on past the large thatched house. The road curves and climbs out of the valley. At the top it bears right. Here a footpath signpost points diagonally across the field on the left. By following this route you reach the gate you saw earlier on your outward journey. It is now a simple matter of retracing your steps to the White Horse Inn.

18 **Parkham**
The Bell Inn

This attractive building is said to date from the 13th century. If this is true then it has stood the test of time remarkably well. The interior has been refurbished considerably and the decor is now rather plush. Carpets and wallpaper give 'style' and modern facilities give comfort. However, the old-world charm has not been lost: traditional wooden furniture, pictures of country scenes and various alcoves retain the character of a village pub. The interior is surprisingly spacious. An open-plan bar room has separate eating areas leading off. One of these acts as a dining room, another as a family room. In winter months woodburning stoves keep the place cosy and warm.

This is a freehouse serving real ales (Draught Bass and Flowers IPA), draught cider (Inch's Stonehouse) and various wines. The food on offer is excellent and cannot be recommended too strongly for its variety and quality. All sorts of bar snacks are available – home-made pâté, soups, filled rolls, jacket potatoes for example – and a range of main meals, like steaks, gammon, meat pies and local trout. Vegetarians can enjoy various pasta and cheese dishes, and daily specials add to the regular choices.

Normal pub opening times are kept. Children are welcome. This is a friendly, welcoming establishment and should not be missed. Telephone: 01237 451201.

How to get there: Parkham stands on a hilltop site just 2 miles from the North Devon coast. Clovelly is 5 miles north-westwards, Bideford is 5 miles north-eastwards. It can easily be reached from Horns Cross, which lies on the A39 Bideford to Bude road. The Bell Inn will be found at the southern edge of the village.

Parking: There is a large pub car park. Vehicles can also be left along the roadside outside – the village lanes are not busy. Extra parking space can be found outside the church, at the northern end of Parkham.

Length of the walk: 2½ miles. Map: OS Landranger sheet 190 Bude and Clovelly (inn GR 388212).

The north-west corner of Devon is surprisingly little known. It is a vast, unpopulated landscape of hills and valleys, woods and hedgerows. The air almost has the tang of Cornwall, with its salty bleakness. The coastline north of Parkham, from Bideford to Hartland, is especially beautiful, with wooded cliffs and forgotten little bays.

This short walk should be seen as just an example of the many walks that can be done in this area. It circles the countryside east of Parkham using farm tracks, footpaths and country lanes. However, one particular stretch is liable to be overgrown in summer months so walkers should be prepared. The views are pleasant throughout.

The Walk

From the Bell Inn walk north to the main part of the village, where the old cottages cluster around the 15th century church. From there, and keeping the church to your left, take the lane that runs straight on, not signposted. Do not take the lane to the right signposted to Bideford and Horns Cross, labelled as 'Unsuitable for Heavy Vehicles'. The road you want goes down by the churchyard wall and turns sharply left. At this point however you continue straight ahead, down a gravel track that runs past a farm. In due course this track becomes grassy. It descends a steep slope, between hedgerows, and offers lovely views ahead, across the rolling hills towards Bideford. Sadly, the sea – which is no distance away – is not quite visible.

At the bottom, beyond a cottage on the left, the track becomes gravel-surfaced again and then meets the road. Turn right. After this road bends, turn left to cross the river Yeo and then right to follow the signs for Parkham and Bradworthy. This road accompanies the river and proceeds southwards up the valley under a dark canopy of trees.

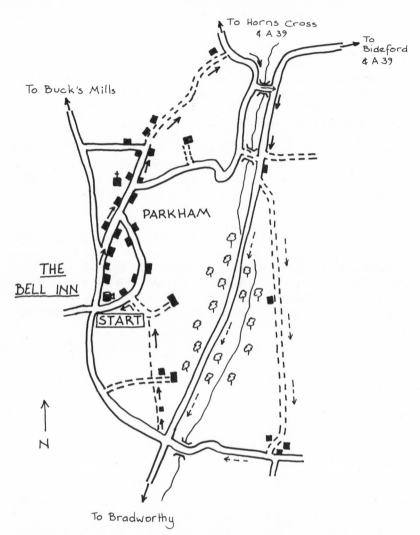

To Horns Cross
& A 39

To Bideford
& A 39

To Buck's Mills

PARKHAM

THE
BELL INN

START

N

To Bradworthy

During the summer months it might be advisable to keep to this road, all the way to the top. The traffic is not very busy and the woods either side give shade and interest. Down to the right flows the river itself, bubbling along on its way to the river Torridge and the Bristol Channel. However, during those times of year when vegetation is not a problem to the intrepid walker an alternative route may be chosen. After a narrow lane to the left, which is unsuitable for long vehicles, you pass a small cottage, also on the left. Immediately after this, on the

78

same side, a grassy track curves up beneath the trees. Follow this. The way is rutted and clear, and runs uphill to reach a small cottage set back behind the hedgerow on the right. Beyond this point the track continues, still between hedgerows as it ascends out of the woodland. This next stretch is that section which can be difficult when the undergrowth has fully grown. The nettles especially can be a problem. But when the weeds are low, the walk can be pleasant. At the very top you emerge at a farmstead, where a bend to the right then left brings you to the road. Turn right.

By either route you reach a crossroads. Turn up the lane that leads to Parkham, that is, westwards. About 100 yards along this lane, on the right, you will see a stile, high in the hedgerow, up a grassy bank. A rough flight of steps leads up to it. Take this path. Beyond the stile follow the field edge to an old barn. There another stile, and gates, lead you onwards. Continue in the same direction along the edge of the next field, keeping the hedgerow to your left. At the farmstead you cross over a track (using another stile on your way) and proceed along a grassy pathway that goes straight on. This runs between hedges and past a house over to the right. At the gravel track soon reached continue in the same direction to meet the road. This is now the southern end of Parkham. The Bell Inn can be reached by turning left.

19 Great Torrington
The Black Horse Inn

This is thought to be one of the oldest inns in Devon, being a tavern long before General Fairfax used the building as his regional headquarters during the Civil War of the 17th century. Much of the original medieval character, thankfully, remains. There are cobbles in the hallway floor, oak beams are found everywhere and some of the walls are panelled. The leaded light windows give the rooms a dark, warm, cosy atmosphere, accentuated in winter by the log fires burning in the grates.

There is a main bar room at the front, which acts as the public bar and the locals' favourite gathering place. A separate lounge, to the right of the entrance, is comfortable and attractively dominated by a grand stone fireplace. The dining room lies at the the back of the building.

This is a Courage house, but the range of real ales on offer would equal anything a freehouse might offer. Five are offered, with the guest beers changing regularly – Wadworths, John Smith's, Webster's . . . The range of wines is equally wide, as indeed is the food served. 'Large and varied' aptly describes the menu. Bar snacks include salads, jacket potatoes, sandwiches (normal and toasted) and soups; main meals include lamb casseroles, chicken burgers, lasagnes, and fish dishes. The steak and kidney pie is much in demand. There are several vegetarian options and children have their own menu.

Normal pub opening times are kept. Being a town centre inn there is no garden but this fact seems hardly to matter.

Telephone: 01805 622121.

How to get there: Great Torrington stands on the east bank of the Torridge river, about 6 miles upstream from Bideford. Barnstaple is 9 miles away to the north-east, Okehampton about 17 miles to the south-east. The Black Horse will be found at the centre of town, almost opposite the Town Hall in the High Street.

Parking: There is no pub car park here. However, there are many public car parks dotted around Torrington, these being the 'pay-and-display' variety. Yellow lines prohibit parking in many of the town's streets.

Length of the walk: 2 miles. Map: OS Landranger sheet 180 Barnstaple and Ilfracombe (inn GR 495192).

Great Torrington is an attractive and interesting town with many ancient buildings and historic associations. The Torridge valley, along this stretch, is deeply cut and the steep slopes are wooded. Elsewhere the countryside immediately around the town has been left as common land, where numerous paths allow walkers to enjoy the flora and fauna of the district. In consequence there are many walks that can be undertaken, and many places to visit.

This short route runs through the town, alongside the river Torridge (following the course of an old canal) and back over the site of the Norman castle, close to where a monument now stands commemorating the Battle of Waterloo. Parts of the journey will be enjoyed especially by those interested in medieval and industrial history.

The Walk

The first stretch of this walk involves going through town and down the hill to Taddiport, a southern suburb that clusters around a bridge over the river Torridge. Turn right outside the Black Horse Inn, right again along South Street and then – where South Street turns right to become Halsdon Terrace – straight on down Mill Street. This winds its way past some old cottages and descends steeply to the river. At the bottom is the old Torridge Inn.

Taddiport is a fascinating little spot. It grew largely as a result of industrialisation and the use of the river Torridge for trade. The stone bridge is 17th century and there are many buildings dating from the early days of the Industrial Revolution. A canal once ran through here

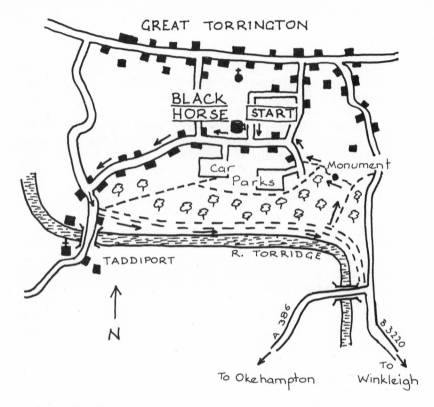

and an old toll house can still be seen. During the Middle Ages there was a leper colony on the far side of the river, on a site now marked by two narrow strip fields. Towering above Taddiport, west of the bridge, is the Dartington Crystal Works, where the famous glass is made. Here there is a visitor centre and factory shop. There are glass making demonstrations also.

The circular walk continues along the Rolle Road – a wide, gravel trackway that runs eastwards from Taddiport along the north bank of the river. This is a very pleasant section, with the Torridge flowing down to the right and the steep wooded slopes up to the left. This was once part of the Rolle Canal, built from 1825 to link Torrington with the sea at Bideford. The Rolle family did much for the town over the years. Apart from financing this waterway it built the Town Mills, re-established the local education system by funding many of the schools, and restored several of Torrington's old buildings. This section of the Rolle Canal was filled in soon after the stretch closed in 1871. For a while, subsequently, it became a toll road.

It is possible to walk along Rolle Road all the way to the Town Bridge, which carries the A386 across the river close to the Town Mills, a former grist mill using water wheels for grinding. But, for this circular walk, you leave the track about two-thirds the way along. The point where you turn left can be identified by a short length of stone, parapet-topped wall which you will see on the right of the track. It is, in fact, a bridge wall, for there is a tributary stream underneath, flowing into the Torridge. Climb the steep, earthy path that runs up beside this tributary stream, through the woodland that covers the valley side. Towards the top this track swings right to meet the road and a flight of steps continues uphill. Take these and turn left along a narrow tarmac path that runs across the slope. This path winds its way up to the top of the slope and will eventually bring you out back near Torrington town centre. On the way it passes the Waterloo Monument, or Obelisk, and the site of medieval Torrington Castle. The latter is delineated by some fragments of wall, a bowling green and the edge of a car park.

The Waterloo Monument, from which there are good views down across the Torridge valley, is a memorial to those who died in that great battle, fought in June 1815. It was erected three years after the battle, and remains one of the favourite resting places for local inhabitants. From here the walk back to the Black Horse is easy – just aim for the spire of Torrington's church.

Bishop's Tawton
The Chichester Arms

Inside, this pub is deceptively large. Not only is there one large, open-plan front bar room but also, beyond, there are various other rooms: a restaurant, family room, function room. At the rear there is also a garden with terrace. But then the Chichester Arms needs to be spacious, it is very popular.

The low ceiling beams, traditional furniture and areas of stone wall maintain the old-world charm. There are horse-brasses hung up and, at one end, a collection of old bottles. The small windows – since this is an ancient building – mean that the interior is liable to be a trifle dark. This is a distinct advantage on hot, sunny days when it is also very cool.

Various real ales are usually available, like Worthington Best and Bass, together with ciders and wines. But it is the food that is especially popular with customers, both in variety and quality. A full range of bar snacks and main meals can be studied in the menu books, kept on the counter, and there are also daily specials written up on the blackboard. There are sandwiches, ploughman's lunches and soups, grills, steaks and fish dishes. The seafood items are especially good.

The Chichester Arms keeps normal pub opening times.

Telephone: 01271 43945.

How to get there: Bishop's Tawton is just 2 miles south of Barnstaple – indeed, it is almost a suburb. The A377 road to Crediton runs through the village. Bideford is 8 miles away to the west, South Molton 10 miles to the east. The Chichester Arms does not, itself, stand on the A377 but on the lane (now bypassed) that acts as the main village street. It is on the corner of the road to Codden.

Parking: There is a pub car park, opposite and down the road a little. Vehicles can also be left along the roadsides of the village, but preferably not along the A377.

Length of the walk: 4 miles. Map: OS Landranger sheet 180 Barnstaple and Ilfracombe (inn GR 567301).

This walk can be divided into two parts. The outward route ascends and descends Codden Hill, upon which stands a monument to Caroline Thorpe. The return route is along a tributary of the river Taw, following a section of the Tarka Trail, a long distance footpath inspired by the famous otter story by Henry Williamson. Thus, there are two kinds of scenery to be enjoyed: upland country with wide views all around, and meadow country with flat pastures and woods. The paths used are very clear and there should be no problem about route-finding.

The Walk

From the village centre walk south, downhill to join the main A377 road, as it trundles along the valley of the river Taw on its way to Crediton. Fortunately, you do not walk along this road for long. Just a few hundred yards ahead on the left is a narrow lane branching off, signposted to Cobbaton Combat Collection and Chittlehampton. At that point, two other routes lead off: an earthy track half-left leading up to a gate and a rutted stony track leading up sharp left. Take the latter. This climbs up under the trees and then bears right, to proceed along a narrow, dark, gully-type passage. The hedgebanks rise high either side and the trees above form an arched canopy.

This clear, much-used track is not, in fact, a public right of way. But it is a route where walkers are permitted, since it climbs steadily to the top of one of the most popular viewpoints in the area – Codden Beacon. The ascent can be steep in parts but the frequent rests, to regain breath, will allow you to enjoy the ever-widening views as you rise above the Taw valley. After leaving the trees behind you find a clear, wide, grassy track running along the ridge of the hill. To the right is a wire fence, beyond which is farmland. To the left is the bracken-covered slope, beyond which are the spreading views over Barnstaple. In due course you can see the monument ahead, marking the summit.

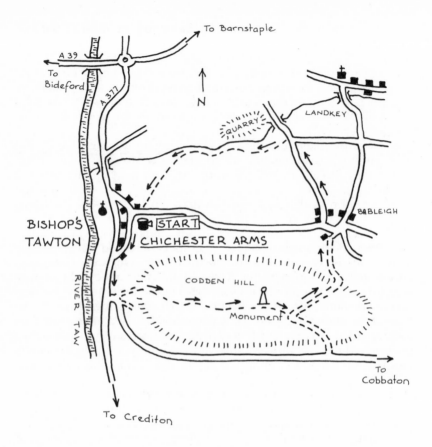

A wooden fence accompanies the track on either side for the last few hundred yards, and a cattle grid protects the monument from grazing animals. Also at the summit is a conveniently placed seat, for the comfortable enjoyment of the glorious views to be had all round. The hill is only 629 feet high but you might imagine it is higher, such is the panorama. The sea is clear to the west, and Exmoor to the northeast. And is that Dartmoor on the southern horizon?

The tall, white concrete monument, surmounted by an ornate stone urn, was erected to the memory of Caroline, wife of Jeremy Thorpe M.P. She lived at nearby Cobbaton and used to love this great eminence. In 1970 a tragic accident led to her premature death, at the age of just 32. It is a sad place – yet an exhilarating one paradoxically, for the whole of North Devon lies below.

The route continues along the clear trackway that continues past the monument, over another cattle grid, and along the crest of the hill. The village of Landkey can be seen down across the valley to your left. In due course you reach a gate, on the far side of which are two paths. One curves round to the right, the other leads down to the left. Follow the latter. This is a pleasant descent: a grassy-stony track bordered by high hedges, winding down gradually to the left. It does not take long to reach the bottom, and to look back up to the green slopes of Codden Beacon.

At the tarmac lane turn right, to go steeply up for a few yards, and then left at the road junction, to go steeply down. The hamlet here, incidentally, is called Bableigh. At the fork, a road sign indicates the left direction as the way to Codden and Bishop's Tawton, and the right direction as that to Venn and Barnstaple. Choosing the latter, continue downhill, keeping to this road for about ½ mile.

Where a road joins from the right (from Landkey) you will see a gate on the left, with an adjoining stile. A notice attached states that the path here is one instigated by the ECC Quarries Company. Furthermore, it is part of the Tarka Trail. The public right of way actually runs along the river, at the base of the local quarry, but this permitted route cuts off that section which runs alongside the rock-faces. It is, therefore, a cut-off willingly to be used. The path thus followed runs over a field, down across a stream and through a thicket, and then right over a stile. At that point you rejoin the public footpath, which now continues along the river bank. This is the Tarka Trail proper.

The Tarka Trail runs for 180 miles and meanders from Exmoor to Dartmoor. It links separate sections of footpaths and passes through some of the loveliest and most unspoilt countryside in Devon. It was instigated by Devon County Council and commemorates the books of Henry Williamson, who lived in the Barnstaple area for many years and wrote affectionately about the North Devon landscape. His most famous book, *Tarka the Otter*, was set in this 'land of the two rivers' (the Taw and Torridge).

The way back to Bishop's Tawton is along a section of the Tarka Trail, and so is well signposted, and well marked by arrow discs. For a while you keep close to the river, crossing two little tributaries on your way and passing through lines of hedgerow. After crossing the second tributary aim diagonally uphill, across two large fields. A gate in the top corner leads out onto the road. Turn right and Bishop's Tawton village is reached almost immediately.

21 Hatherleigh
The George Hotel

What a wonderfully old and interesting building this is! Set around a central, cobbled courtyard it consists of a jumble of doors and windows leading into a series of rooms at different levels. Everywhere there are bare stone walls and low beamed ceilings. Many of the rooms form part of the hotel complex; the pub section being found at the rear, reached most easily from the car park (beyond the courtyard). This is called the Jubilee Bar. Here there is a large brick fireplace and, down some steps, a separate section where stands the pool table.

Back in the 14th century this fascinating building was a retreat house and sanctuary for the monks of Tavistock Abbey. After the Reformation, however – when monastic property was confiscated by the Crown and various 'favoured' aristocrats – it became a brew house and tavern, doubling also as a local law court. By the 18th century it was a well known coaching inn, a popular stop-over point for London to Penzance travellers.

Today the George Inn is still well-known – now for its hospitality, old-world cosiness and for the quality of its food. It is a freehouse, serving many different real ales (including Otter, Boddingtons and Bass), several draught ciders (like Inch's Stonehouse) and various wines. The food offered is equally wide-ranging, the large blackboards over the fireplace listing all manner of tempting dishes. There are snacks (such as soup, sandwiches, pasties, ploughman's lunches); succulent starters (such as squid, oysters, garlic mushrooms); main courses (such as meat pies, seafood platters, lasagnes, salads); and puddings (such as lemon soufflé and crème caramel). The George Inn is especially proud of its fish dishes. Vegetarians are well served too, with vegetable and pasta bakes.

The Jubilee Bar keeps normal pub opening times, although drinks are available all day in the hotel section of the George.

Telephone: 01837 810454.

How to get there: Hatherleigh stands in the heart of that undiscovered part of Devon wedged between Dartmoor, Exmoor and Cornwall. It is 7 miles north-west of Okehampton, 20 miles south of Barnstaple, 24 miles east of Bude. The A386 Great Torrington to Tavistock road passes through, as does the A3072 Holsworthy to Crediton road. The George Hotel will be found at the upper (northern) end of town, close to the church.

Parking: There is a large pub car park, but this is reached not through the courtyard but from the market place behind the building. This car park stands next to a large public car park, also next to the market.

Length of the walk: 4 miles. Map: OS Landranger sheet 191 Okehampton and North Dartmoor (inn GR 542045).

No book of this kind, covering North Devon, should omit Hatherleigh. It is an old, attractive, quiet little town situated on a steep slope overlooking the river Lew, a tributary of the Torridge. There are many ancient buildings (apart from the George Hotel) and the countryside all around is beautiful.

This walk offers a taste of this countryside, circling the area immediately to the east of Hatherleigh. The route includes meadow and river scenery, rolling farmlands and even some moorland. From Hatherleigh Monument there are, in addition, superb views southwards, to the Dartmoor skyline. The paths, bridleways and tracks used are clear throughout and there are many signposts to show the way.

The Walk

The route begins through the town southwards, so turn right outside the front entrance of the George Hotel and walk down the main street. The church, which stands at the top of the hill, will be passed at the end of the circuit.

Hatherleigh is popular amongst anglers, for the river Lew flows across the meadows below the town, the river Torridge flows just

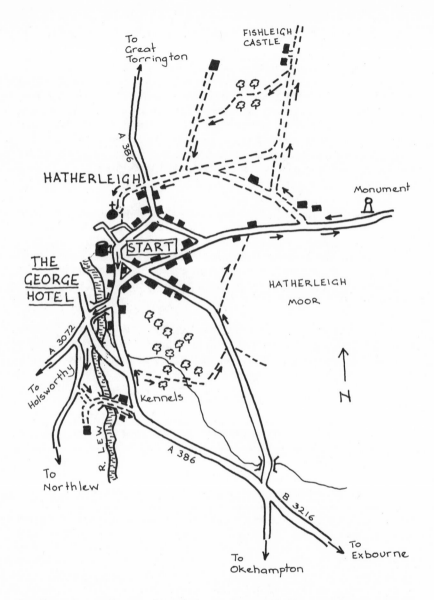

1 mile away to the north and the Hole Brook flows along the valley 2 miles eastward. Yet it is not just anglers who come here. The livestock market every Tuesday brings many visitors, as do the pottery, art gallery, craft and antique shops and teashops.

At the bottom of the hill, beyond the Bridge Inn turn right to go over the bridge, across the bypass and along the A3072 road signposted to Highampton and Holsworthy. Then, after about 300 yards, turn left along a narrow lane. This is signposted to Northlew. After another 300 yards or so turn left again, this time along a narrower lane. The Hatherleigh Methodist Church cemetery stands at the corner here. There now follows a pleasant stroll, between hedges, to a ford and footbridge across the river Lew itself. On the way take care to keep left where the track for Passaford Farm goes off to the right. Beyond the footbridge, where the Lew flows attractively under the trees, continue past the cottages (in fact, the Riverside Boarding Kennels and Cattery) to join the main road. Turn left, as if to return to Hatherleigh.

Happily you do not stay on the main road for long. Opposite the sports field and immediately before the stone bridge over a stream, turn right. There is a gate here and a footpath sign pointing the way. Cross the field diagonally half-right to the far corner where a path continues through a little wood. Through the trees on your right is an open field. Using the wooden footbridge, with steps either end, cross the stream and continue in the same direction as before. Leaving the trees behind aim for the far corner of the field. There, two gates present themselves. Choose the one on the right. Beyond this the path swings left, to cross an area of grass and bracken. On the far side is a gate to the road. By this time you are walking over Hatherleigh Moor, an area of rough grazing, gorse and bracken. It is an interesting, rather wild area and rich in both flora and fauna.

On the road – a quiet country lane in fact – turn left and then, very shortly after, right along a bridleway, which you reach through a gate. This track now leads you through the gorse and then up across a grassy field towards the building on the skyline. This brings you onto another lane, close to a house called Yollaberry. Turn right and walk along this lane to the locally-famous Monument.

This tall, granite obelisk was erected in 1860 in memory of Lieutenant-Colonel William Morris, a local man, who fought so bravely at the Charge of the Light Brigade, 1854, during the Crimean War. The Bronze relief at the base of the monument shows Morris being carried from the battlefield. Close by is a panorama and information board, for this is also a popular viewpoint. On clear days the Dartmoor skyline includes Yes Tor, The Belstone Tors and – at 2,037 feet the highest point of the moor – High Wilhays.

Leaving the monument back the way you came (westwards) turn right up a track past a bungalow. This track changes from a tarmac one to an earthy one and bears right. Ignore the grassy track that continues westward, here, which is private. Now walking north you keep to this track as it descends, to meet a tarmac lane, coming in from the left.

Follow this lane, northward still, to Fishleigh Castle. This is not a castle, in fact, but a farm. All around are views across the hills of North Devon and time should be spent appreciating the scene. There are not many places in England as unspoilt as this.

Just before the farm buildings you will see a stile, and a footpath sign, on the left. The way back to Hatherleigh is now clear. Cross the field diagonally (away from the farm) to the top corner, where a stile leads into the next field, where you continue in the same direction. In the bottom corner of that field a path takes you through a copse of trees, over a footbridge and up to a stile. Following the edge of the next field (with the hedge on the left) the final stile leads onto a gravel track. Turn left and follow this all the way back to the northern end of Hatherleigh (turning right at a T-junction beforehand).

At Hatherleigh cross the main road to walk down the lane to the church. Now is the time to look inside, for it is a fine 15th century building, containing a Norman font, a wall painting of St Christopher and some Jacobean pews. The George Hotel will be found on the far side of the churchyard, just round the corner.

North Tawton
22 The Copper Key Inn

This building was already more than a hundred years old when it became, during the English Civil War in the mid 17th century, a base for Royalist troops. At that time the Copper Key was something of a local sports centre – for cock fighting and bare-knuckle boxing, that is. It was an ale and cider house and naturally became the focal point for all the young bloods of the village.

Today it is rather more peaceful, but no less popular. Overnight accommodation is provided: there are separate rooms for games and families; facilities are offered for private functions, and an excellent range of food and drink is always available. No wonder the Copper Key Inn is the favourite haunt for local businessmen, villagers and tourists alike.

This is a freehouse opening normal pub times. Real ales include Bass and London Pride (although there are periodic changes in this choice), the draught cider is Inch's and there are over 50 wines on the wine list. Teas and coffees are also available. In the main bar, various snacks and meals are served, like ploughman's lunches, triple-decker sandwiches, jacket potatoes, things with chips, curries, lasagnes and fish dishes; in the separate restaurant there is an à la carte menu with various meat and fish specials. Chidren are given their own menu, and the puddings are suitably fattening. Vegetarians can have a vegetable curry, nut bake or a 'seaweed basket'.

This is a cosy, friendly place. The low beams; the traditional furniture; the brass and copper ware decorating the walls; the separate rooms divided from the main bar area by steps down to a lower level – all help to give the Copper Key an intimate feel.

Telephone: 01837 82357.

How to get there: Many people say that North Tawton is the geographical centre of Devon. It is certainly in the middle of nowhere! No large towns are anywhere near: Exeter is nearly 20 miles away (eastwards), Barnstaple nearly 25 miles away (northwards). Amongst smaller towns Okehampton is the nearest, 7 miles away to the south-west. This small, attractive town – or large village – stands just off the A3072 Hatherleigh to Crediton road. The Copper Key Inn will be found at the western end, close to the bridge over the river Taw.

Parking: There is a pub car park opposite, and vehicles can also be left in various places, along the roads and side turnings of the town.

Length of the walk: 4 miles. Map: OS Landranger sheet 191 Okehampton and North Dartmoor (inn GR 657018).

This walk actually circles the pub. It combines a stroll along the Taw riverbank with a perambulation of North Tawton itself. From Bouchers Hill, just north of the town, there are also some splendid views to be had – especially southward to Dartmoor. Some may choose to undertake only half the distance, since the route can easily be sub-divided into two separate 2 mile circular walks.

The paths are clearly signposted throughout and, for the most part, are well-trodden. However there are stiles to be climbed, and some steep slopes to negotiate.

The Walk

Turn right outside the Copper Key and walk down the road to the bridge over the river Taw. Immediately over this, on the left, is a footpath signpost and metal turnstile gate. Here begins the walk.

The route for the next mile needs little description. You simply follow the river along, southwards (that is, upstream). To the left, across the river itself, the ground rises to North Tawton, the buildings being seen on the skyline. To the right, across the meadows, is the large cheese factory. And straight ahead, on the distant horizon, are the dark slopes of Dartmoor. This is a pleasant stretch. The path winds

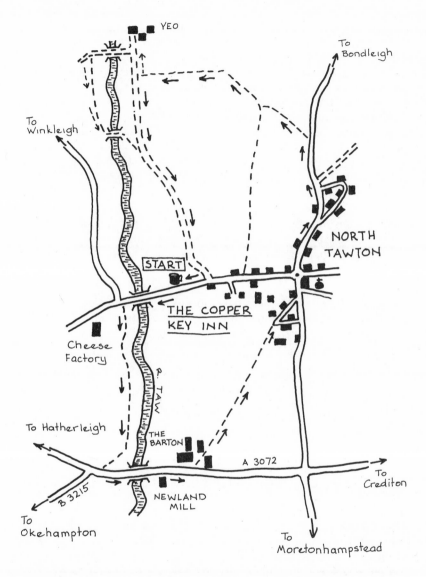

YEO

To Bondleigh

To Winkleigh

NORTH TAWTON

START

THE COPPER KEY INN

Cheese Factory

R. TAW

To Hatherleigh

THE BARTON

A 3072

To Crediton

B 3215

NEWLAND MILL

To Okehampton

To Moretonhampstead

around with the meanders, goes through a number of gates and runs along the edges of several fields. In due course both river and path bear right and you meet the road. Turn left. Follow this main road eastward a short way: over a bridge, past Newland Mill on the right and past The Barton on the left. The latter is a splendid building, being a large, stone-built and thatched edifice with mullioned windows. It

95

is Tudor in date. At the end of the wall that surrounds The Barton's garden turn left, to walk through a gravel yard. The vast agricultural buildings behind The Barton are now used for agro-industrial purposes, but there is neither noise nor smell. Keeping these buildings to your left, you soon reach the edge of open fields again. North Tawton can be seen ahead.

The footpath back is clear and much-used by locals. It cuts diagonally across two large fields, passing through a gate on its way. At the corner of the second field a stile leads through to a grassy track, that runs up to the houses of an estate. On the tarmac road continue straight on, past the little police and fire stations. Turn left at the end, to reach the main road junction and town centre. At the middle is an attractive clock tower.

Those wanting merely to do a 2 mile circular walk can turn left at the clock tower, to walk down the hill back to the Copper Key. Those wanting to do the full 4 mile circular walk should take the turning signposted to Bondleigh. This is called North Street and runs past the Ring of Bells public house towards the United Reformed Church. In due course this road bends left, passing the Gospel Hall and Victoria Cottages, to climb Bouchers Hill as it leaves town. At the top, as this road levels off, a footpath signpost will be seen on the left, next to a wide double set of farm gates. There is also a stile here.

Take the direction indicated by the arrow disc. This leads through a gravel yard, round a barn and across a field at an angle. Along this stretch the shallow valley should be down below on the left and, beyond on the horizon, should be the Dartmoor outline. Through the next gate and stile continue in the same direction, across the top of the next field. The following stile has two arrow discs, one pointing left, the other half-right. Follow the latter. This route takes you across two more fields, all the while Dartmoor (and now the cheese factory, which has become visible below) remaining in sight to your left. Climbing over another fence and stile you head down into a valley, along the bottom of which you follow a hedgerow. This leads to yet another stile and then a path within the hedgerow, continuing down in the same direction. At the bottom is a tarmac lane, which is, in fact, a farm track. The aforementioned route across the fields may sound difficult but arrow discs, nailed upon each stile, show the way quite clearly.

The quick way back to the Copper Key is left along the farm track and right at its southern end. But there is an attractive little detour here. Turn right to reach the farmstead at Yeo, then cross the river Taw to return along its west bank, across the meadows. This brings you to a footbridge and back across the river to the tarmac track, where you rejoin the official route.

Zeal Monachorum
The Waie Inn

This inn has been converted from a farmhouse – the Waie Farm once being a large mixed farm spreading along the Taw valley. The conversion has been done well, the rooms now offering modern facilities in traditional surroundings. Apart from being a pub, a restaurant and a venue for large private functions, the Waie Inn also acts as a sports and leisure centre. There is a heated swimming pool, a gym and sauna, plus facilities for squash, snooker, table tennis, skittles and pool. Perhaps not surprisingly the place is open all day and has some of the feel of a leisure centre, in its internal atmosphere. There are many different rooms, the carpets and decor are free from clutter and people can be heard enjoying themselves in the far corners of the building. The furniture is mainly pine, of the bench and settle variety. There are two main bar rooms, one acting as a public bar, the other as a lounge.

But those not of a sporting nature should not be put off – for the Waie is extremely friendly and welcoming. The choice of drinks is wide and the food is excellent. It is a freehouse serving real ales (like Bass and Ruddles), draught cider (Inch's and Dry Blackthorn), and wines (like Englefield's). The food consists of the usual pub variety –

but this is well presented and reasonably priced. There are snacks such as sandwiches, ploughman's lunches and so on, and main meals like steak, fish and salad. But it is the roast dinner on which the Waie especially prides itself. All in all – this is certainly the place to go.
Telephone: 01363 82348.

How to get there: Zeal Monachorum stands 7 miles north-west of Crediton, and 11 miles north-east of Okehampton. There is no main road here. The village will be found between the A377 (from Barnstaple) and the A3072 (from Hatherleigh), west of where these roads meet at Copplestone. The Waie Inn is located at the southern end of Zeal, down the hill from the church.

Parking: There is a large car park at the Waie. There is, in addition, plenty of space for roadside parking at this end of the village.

Length of the walk: 4½ miles. Map: OS Landranger sheet 191 Okehampton and North Dartmoor (inn GR 722037).

Zeal Monachorum is sited on the river Yeo. This is not the famous Yeo, of course, that flows in Somerset through Yeovil, but the one that rises at the northern fringe of Dartmoor and flows down to meet the river Taw at Lapford, just 3 miles away northwards. It is a pretty river, with a lovely winding valley, running between wooded hills. The outward journey of this walk follows the river down its course, along the river bank. The return follows the river back up its course, this time at a higher level. Thus, the valley can be seen from different perspectives. The walk also takes in the pretty village of Down St Mary, from where there are views across to Dartmoor.

The paths used are clearly marked throughout. However, depending upon time of year some sections may become slightly overgrown.

The Walk

If you turn left outside the Waie Inn, and follow the lane that leads up beside the garden, you will, in due course, reach the river Yeo, down amongst the trees at the bottom of the valley. Immediately after crossing the bridge at that point turn left. The gate in front leads into an old quarry. The little path that leads off to the left, however, runs along the river bank and then emerges on the far side of this quarry. This is the route to be used – for a short walk through the trees is preferable to a short walk through a quarry.

At the far side of the quarry a track leads onwards to reach a gate. Beyond this the path continues, along the bottom edge of a field. The woods that hug the river banks are to your left and all around (and above you) are the little hills that cluster about the Yeo valley. This is

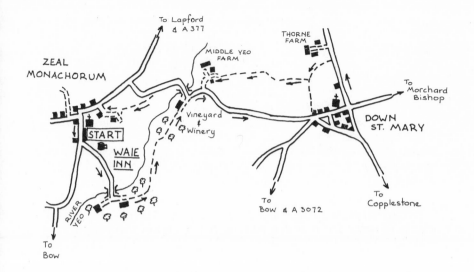

a lovely stretch, and very easy to follow. Keep close to the river at first, along the edges of two fields, and then follow the path as it gains height, to contour through a pine wood. At the end of the trees you continue in the same direction, returning to the river bank for a while before another gate and stile leads on towards the distant farm buildings. There, a grassy track goes past an open-sided barn to a further stile, close to a thatched house. Thence a tarmac lane takes you to the road.

This thatched house, and accompanying buildings, is actually part of the Down St Mary Vineyard and Winery where visitors are welcome to taste and buy its produce. You will be passing this happy site again later in the walk.

On the road, continue eastwards, following the tarmac as it climbs out of the valley. This road takes you all the way to the village of Down St Mary – and the route is uphill all the way. Down St Mary happens to be a hill-top settlement. The 'Down' is a corruption of 'dun' which was Saxon for 'hill', although – judging from its position, on a naturally defensive site – its foundation is probably older, Celtic perhaps. Today it is a pleasant village, clustering around a small triangular green. There are wide views all round, with Dartmoor to the south.

The way back to Zeal Monachorum begins a short way north of the 15th century church. Keeping left as you reach the village green, turn left at the corner of the churchyard. This lane takes you past Marydowne House, which is on the left. A little further on, also on the left, is Thorne Farm. The right of way once led directly from Thorne Farm westwards to Middle Yeo Farm. But this has now been changed officially. Leaving the road, on the left, shortly before Thorne Farm the path has been redirected around a number of fields, and over a number of stiles. The route is made clear with directional indicators. At Middle Yeo Farm follow the track up to the left, to join the road. Turn right to walk down to the vineyard mentioned earlier.

Now continue along the road as it crosses the bridge, bends left and climbs the valley side. A little way before the top is a footpath signpost on the left, pointing the way across a stile. The footpath from here leads directly to Zeal but this is a section that can be difficult, depending upon the time of year. If in doubt, continue along the road, turning left at the T-junction. The footpath begins by leading along the far side of the hedgerow that bounds the road – in other words, by running parallel with the road, to its left. The valley of the Yeo is way down to your left and, upon the slope immediately to your left, is the vineyard owned by the Down St Mary Winery. At the far top corner a stile, next to a telegraph pole, takes you into the next field. Continue in the same direction with the hedge still to your right. Where this hedge ends, in the following field, cut down, to cross a side valley – by this time a shallow combe, for you have been following it upstream. There, in the bottom hedge, you will find a stile. Once over this, head steeply uphill to join and then follow the hedgerow as it curves up to a gate. Through this a track leads to the right, to wind through some farm buildings to the road. You are now at the top end of Zeal Monachorum. Turn left to walk past the 14th century church and down to the Waie Inn.

24 Chawleigh
The Chilcott Arms

This freehouse prides itself not only on its range of drinks, but on its food. And well it might. Half the building is given over to a restaurant where a full à la carte menu is offered; the other half (the 'pub' end) offers a wide range of bar snacks. And excellent all this food is, both in quality and value for money. Working up from sandwiches, ploughman's lunches and omelettes, there are things with chips, salads, steaks, fish dishes and a range of vegetarian courses. The fish items are especially popular, and lobster is served in season.

The interior decor is traditional, with a strong homely feel. Under a low ceiling and set about a stone surround bar counter, the furniture is comfortable rather than 'olde worlde'. There are pictures on the walls and some antiques dotted around. Outside – to one side of the building – is a pleasant little garden with tables and chairs.

Normal pub opening times are kept. The real ales offered include Bass, Dartmoor and Exmoor Stag, and the draught cider has the choice of Blackthorn or a local scrumpy. As befitting a pub-cum-restaurant, there is also a full wine list.

The Chilcott Arms is a friendly place where everyone is made to feel welcome, including families with children.

Telephone: 01769 580204.

How to get there: Chawleigh stands in central Devon, midway between Exmoor and Dartmoor. It is 8 miles south of South Molton, 14 miles west of Tiverton, 12 miles north-east of Okehampton. The B3042 road runs through the village on its way from Chulmleigh to Witheridge. The Chilcott Arms will be found south of the church.

Parking: There is a pub car park. Vehicles may also be left around the village where space allows, especially near the church which stands back from the main road.

Length of the walk: 4 miles. Map: OS Landranger sheet 180 Barnstaple and Ilfracombe (inn GR 712125).

The hills and valleys of central Devon are still, fortunately, undiscovered by the great mass of tourists. They are still, therefore, totally unspoilt – making them perfect for the walker and country lover. This walk wanders around one particular valley – that of the Little Dart, a river that rises on Witheridge Moor and flows to the river Taw near Chulmleigh. It has a lovely, winding, wooded valley dotted about with farms and hamlets.

The bridleways and footpaths used are not well signposted, neither are they, in parts, well trodden. But the route, nevertheless, is clear.

The Walk

Turning left outside the Chilcott Arms, take the lane signposted to Cheldon and Gidley Arms. This leads all the way down to the bottom of the valley, where it crosses the bridge over the Little Dart river. Then turn left, continuing along the lane to Gidley Arms and past Stone Mill Farm. At the hairpin bend, where the lane turns sharply right, to climb out of the valley, go straight on along a concrete and grass trackway. This leads westwards along the north side of the valley.

This first stretch, about 1 mile in all, is along a public road but it is not a busy road and enjoyment of the scenery should not be lessened by any great amount of traffic. And the scenery is certainly beautiful: an undulating landscape of hills, valleys and woods. This Little Dart river should not be confused with the Dart river that flows down to Bickleigh Mill near Tiverton, nor with the famous Dart that has given its name both to Dartmoor and Dartmouth. 'Dart' is a very common river name in England. It derives from the old Celtic word 'derva' meaning 'oak'. The oak tree once dominated our primeval forests and rivers flowing through oak woodland would often be named after the vegetation of their valleys. The river names Derwent and Darent derive from the same root and are also commonly found.

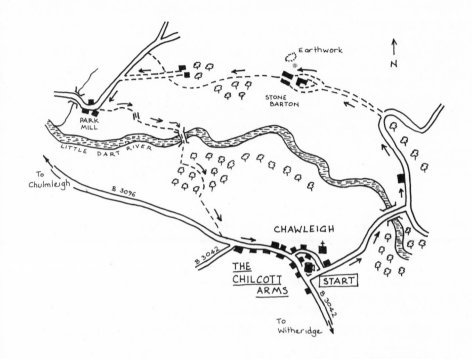

The concrete and grass trackway leads over an old cattle grid and, further on, past a bungalow set back a little to the right. It then climbs the valley side at an angle to Stone Barton. At the fork shortly before the farm buildings, take the concrete way up to the right and not the tarmac way to the left. This leads up above the buildings, skirting them to your left, before descending back to the farmyard at the far side of the house. On your way around Stone Barton cast your eye upwards to the right. On the hillside may be seen the earthworks of the 13th century fortification that has given the farmstead here its name.

Between two lines of cattle sheds you continue to the end of the farmyard where a grassy track leads on between hedgerows. Follow this as it leads along the top edge of a woodland eventually to a gate. Across a little track running downhill go through another gate and continue in the same direction. By this time the path is narrow, running between lines of thicket. Over a tributary stream by stepping stones and through another gate you now cross an open field. Emerging from the trees means you can appreciate more fully the landscape over to the left, where the Little Dart valley winds its wooded way into the distance.

Keeping roughly parallel with the Little Dart river below you curve slightly right as you cross the field. On the far side a gate leads through to another grassy, hedge-bound track. Follow this now all the way to a concrete farm track, curving right as you go. This stretch can be muddy, due to the churning of horses' hooves, but the way is very clear. Once onto the farm track you could, if you wish, continue on the far side along a continuation of the track as it climbs steadily, eventually meeting the road. It is easier, however, to turn left along the farm track to meet the same road further down.

Once on the road turn left, to follow it all the way down to the valley bottom, where begins the footpath back to Chawleigh. Do not cross the river at the bottom, which is a tributary of the Little Dart. As the road bends right beforehand turn left, through a gate immediately before a house called Park Mill. Follow the edge of the field eastwards, keeping the hedgerow to your right. Near the far corner a stile in that hedgerow leads through to a path that runs through some thicket and over two small footbridges. These in fact cross the old leat, that once fed water to the mill further back. Emerging from the thicket, the grassy meadows stretch out in front. Cross these at an angle, aiming all the while for the far corner. Soon you meet the Little Dart river itself on your right and, almost immediately thereafter, the footbridge that will carry you across it. This footbridge is a grand affair. Tall brick-built steps take you up to a sturdy wooden construction some 20 yards long. No danger of getting your feet wet here!

On the far side bear slightly right, to cross the meadow towards the corner of a little woodland. At that corner, on your left, is a gate. Through this is the grassy track that leads up through the wood. Take this. A fairly steep climb, but not an unpleasant one, brings you to a gate, at the top edge of the trees. Through this bear left, to follow a clear grassy path running along the top of a little valley, which is down to your left. This path curves a bit but leads directly to the road at the western end of Chawleigh. Turn left for the Chilcott Arms.

25 North Molton
The Poltimore Inn

Like the village, this pub shows little evidence of its past – for today it is quiet, well-appointed and welcoming to visitors. North Molton was once a mining settlement, and the area all around was pitted with copper, lead and iron ore workings. The inns here served the resident mining population and, during the 19th century in particular, must have been basic indeed.

Now the Poltimore Inn is a listed building and caters for tourists as well as residents. Inside there is one main room, dominated by a long bar counter. One end acts as a public bar, the other as a lounge. Beyond the former is a separate room with a pool table. There is a beamed ceiling, traditional wooden furniture and a large stone fireplace. Old pictures are hung on the walls, and there are ornaments dotted around.

Belonging to the Discovery Inns company, this pub keeps normal pub opening times. The real ales served include Flowers Original and Bass, draught cider is offered and a full range of wines (from 'house wine to champagne'). There is also a good selection of food, from bar snacks like sandwiches to full meals like grills, roasts, steaks and salads. House specialities include Chinese crispy duck and local Exmoor trout, and there are always things on the menu for vegetarians – lasagne, perhaps, macaroni cheese or vegetable curry.

This is a friendly place, ever busy and always full of the noise of happy conversation.

Telephone: 015984 338.

How to get there: North Molton stands, not surprisingly, north of South Molton, by about 3 miles. It is close to the southern boundary of the Exmoor National Park. Barnstaple is 12 miles to the west, Tiverton 18 miles to the south-east. The village does not stand on a main road but can be reached easily from the A361 and A399, roads that join near South Molton. The Poltimore Inn will be found opposite the church, by the village square.

Parking: There is no pub car park but vehicles can be left in the village square, opposite the pub's main entrance. Roadside parking is also possible throughout North Molton, where space permits.

Length of the walk: 3 miles. Map: OS Landranger sheet 180 Barnstaple and Ilfracombe (inn GR 737298).

This is a most attractive walk, down the valley of the river Mole and back. The outward journey is along a footpath which runs across the meadows next to the river. The return journey is along a clear, gravel farm track that contours along the valley side. The route is very clear throughout. After wet weather, however, the meadows are liable to be a trifle damp underfoot. There are a few stiles to climb, and a few gates to open but nothing exists to diminish your full enjoyment of the scenery.

The Walk

The route begins through North Molton itself, downhill from the Poltimore Inn in an easterly direction. A little way down, on the right, you will see the Miners Arms, another popular pub locally. The name of this one, of course, recalls the history of the village.

North Molton may be called a village now but it was very much a town in centuries past. During the Middle Ages it grew wealthy with the wool trade, becoming a borough in its own right. Then, with the advent of the Industrial Revolution, mining helped prosperity – and growth – continue. The iron, lead and copper deposits that had been worked for centuries began to be exploited on a large scale, especially a few miles to the north. A mineral tramway was built along the Mole valley, linking the mines near Heasley Mill with the main railway at South Molton, and all across the district miners' cottages, chapels and pubs sprang up.

A little further down from the Miners Arms, also to the right, a gravel

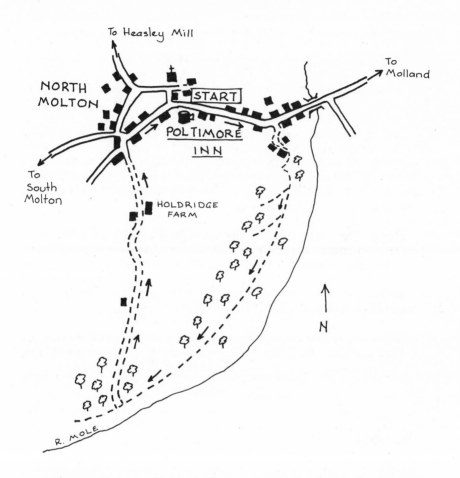

track leads off, immediately before a thatched cottage. A signpost opposite calls it a footpath. And so it is. It will take you past some houses, round a bend or two and will lead you directly to the river Mole. This is the way you want.

Beyond the last house along this track, the way narrows to a path running between hedges. In due course this path bends right, crosses a small stream and bends left to regain its former direction. It is a very clear path, and a very attractive one, offering glimpses of the Mole valley through the trees to the left. Beyond the next gate continue in the same direction, choosing the left in each case of two forks. The paths leading off to the right wander up to the woods but the one you choose runs down to a stile and thence across the open meadows.

The route now is easy and requires no further explanation. You continue in a southerly direction with the river Mole to your left and the woodlands up to your right. Here and there you come close to the river itself, so you can accompany the bubbling water as it gurgles its way towards South Molton. This is a lovely walk. The path wanders over the meadow grasses and between shrubs and tall, young willow trees. In spring and summer the valley is alive with wild flowers: a positive botanist's delight.

After about 1½ miles you reach a gate, beyond which a clear gravel track leads up through the trees on the right. It curves back a little and is deeply sunk between hedgebanks. This is the way back to North Molton. At first it ascends steeply, but the gradient diminishes as it rises out the valley. The surface steadily improves also, from rough stones and gravel at the beginning to tarmac at the end, having passed a couple of farmsteads on the way. The route is naturally clear, and very pretty. Over the hedgerow to the right, are views across the Mole valley and, beyond Holdridge Farm, is a splendid view of North Molton across the fields.

This track emerges at the western end of North Molton. Turn right to walk uphill back to the Poltimore Inn. But, before returning to the pub, you may wish to spend a little time exploring the 15th century church. It boasts some fine panelling and some very interesting monuments. Interestingly, one of these monuments commemorates Sir Amyas Bampfylde, who lived in Elizabethan times. He was part of the great Devon family that established the Baron Poltimore line – hence the name of the local pub.

26 Oakford
The Red Lion Hotel

This is a village pub par excellence: small, friendly and unpretentious. There are two main rooms, one on the left as you enter where the pool table lives, and the bar on the right which doubles also as a lounge. The decor is simple yet interesting. There is a high level plate shelf, with ornaments, and old farming implements adorn the walls. Close to the bar counter is a large inglenook fireplace, which is ablaze with logs during winter months. In short, it has a cosy, comfortable atmosphere which gives a pleasant welcome.

As a freehouse it offers a selection of real ales (including Flowers Original, Hook Norton and Boddingtons) and some excellent draught cider (a barrel of which sits on the bar top). And the choice of food is good too. A regular menu offers the standard fare, like ploughman's lunches, salads, chicken wings, steaks and fish dishes, whilst specialities are chalked up on the blackboards. The spare ribs are good, and the Hawaiian salad should delight the gourmet.

The Red Lion keeps normal pub opening times. Families are welcome and there is a beer garden through the side gateway. As an hotel, it also offers accommodation and there can be few better places to stay if you like simple hospitality and attractive surroundings.

Telephone: 013985 219.

How to get there: Oakford stands in that little known part of North Devon south of Dulverton in Somerset. It is 6 miles north-west of Tiverton and 12 miles east of South Molton. The village does not stand on a main road but can most easily be reached from the A361, or else from the A396 running down the Exe valley. Motorists should take the B3227 road westwards from near Bampton. The Red Lion will be found on the north side of the village street, opposite the lane to the church.

Parking: There is a small pub car park on the opposite side of the village street. Cars can also be left, here and there, along the roadsides but Oakford is small and the lanes in this part of Devon are naturally steep and narrow.

Length of the walk: 3 ½ miles. Map: OS Landranger sheet 181 Minehead and Brendon Hills (inn GR 909213).

This is a beautiful area with deep wooded valleys, rolling hills, narrow lanes almost lost amongst the hedgerows, and isolated villages and hamlets, where time seems to have stood still. This walk takes in two pretty combes, where fast little streams tumble through a landscape of pine trees and steep-sloping pastures. The route is very clear, using footpaths across fields and forest trackways. However, some steep gradients are encountered and, along one particular section, a long flight of log steps must be descended. Elsewhere there are stiles and narrow footbridges to be crossed.

The Walk
The first ½ mile of the route is westwards along the road, so from outside the Red Lion turn right and walk uphill. Very soon you leave the village behind and the views all around open out. This road is, in fact, a quiet country lane almost devoid of traffic so the walk is very pleasant indeed. Simply admire the scenery and enjoy the wild flowers in the hedgerows.

Those with time should look around Oakford first. Situated on the side of a steep hill, it consists of a collection of old cottages, general shop, a village hall (down the road a little way) and a handsome church boasting a 15th century tower. Many guide books eulogize about the place, and rightly so. They commend its location, its timelessness and the fact that the old Devon dialect can still be heard here.

Not long after the road has levelled off, at the top of the hill, you reach a junction. Continue straight on, following the direction signposted to Spurway and Rackenford. Happily this route is also signposted as being unsuitable for heavy goods vehicles. Not, in fact, that you will be on this road for long. Within just a few hundred yards the road bends sharply left, to go downhill, at which point you will

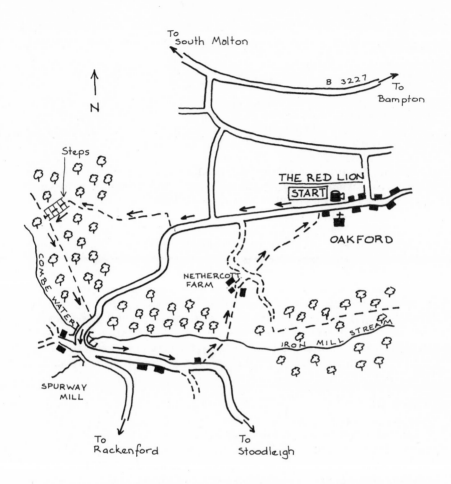

see a gate to your right and a footpath signpost. Take this path. At first it runs along a field edge, with the hedge on your right, to another gate. Thereafter it turns left to follow another field edge, this time with the hedge on your left. Beyond the next gate the path bears half-right, to run diagonally across the field down to the bottom corner, where a stile leads the path into a woodland. All along this stretch arrow discs, nailed upon gate posts, show the way.

The route now leads steeply downhill, through woodland, into the valley of Combe Water. Just a few yards below the stile you reach the top of a long flight of steps cut into the hillside, which runs down to your left. The descent is precipitous, but perfectly safe. The steps have been well constructed out of sawn logs and compacted earth. The rises and treads are firm, if a little irregular. At the bottom, but still high above the stream which babbles below, a clear forest trackway runs across, along the valley side. Turn left along this and, keeping Combe Water down to your right, follow it all the way to the road. You emerge just above Spurway Mill, to which you descend.

This is a delightful spot, where two wooded valleys meet, three country lanes converge and all is quiet, save for the gurgle of the water. Keep to the left as you cross the two little bridges and take the narrow lane signposted to Stoodleigh. This is the lane closest to the Iron Mill stream, whose valley runs eastward from here, to meet the river Exe near Bampton. At the confluence with the Exe is an attractive, chain bridge, dating from the early years of industrialisation. This walk, of course, does not go that far, but a separate visit might be worthwhile. The Iron Mill stream has a valley that would repay further exploration.

On this walk you now leave the road after about ½ a mile, having passed Bellbrook Farm on the right. Immediately after the farm you pass on the left, and before the road turns sharply right, you go through the gate on your left. Cross the meadow field diagonally, away from the farm buildings, and you will find a narrow footbridge (with rail). It is almost hidden by trees in the corner of the field. In fact, there are two footbridges here going over the Iron Mill stream, one after the other. Having crossed both, strike uphill across the gorse-covered grassy field, keeping the woodland over to your left. For a while the path becomes clearer, turning into a tractor-rutted track. At the top, a gate and stile lead you through to the next field, across which you aim for the distant farm buildings (in fact, Nethercott Farm). Another gate now takes you onto a farm track, along which you walk, keeping the farmhouse to your left.

Leaving Nethercott behind, the track becomes a tarmac lane. Very soon this bears left as it climbs out of the valley. At this point another track, this one grassy and earthy, leads off to the right. Here you have a choice. The easy walk back to Oakford is to continue up the tarmac lane to the road at the top and then turn right. The shorter and more pleasant way back is to cut the corner off by taking the footpath across the fields. For the latter route go down the earthy track a short way and bear left through a gate. Follow the edges of two fields and then cut diagonally across a third to a gate and stile at the far side. This brings you out at the road just above Oakford. The Red Lion awaits.

Bickleigh
The Trout Inn

Being located in a popular tourist centre – Bickleigh Mill is a local 'honeypot' – this pub opens all day (11 am – 11 pm) every day except Sundays (when more normal pub opening times are maintained). This is just as well, for the Trout Inn's hospitality is much in demand. There is a wide range of food and drink, a large menu and acres of space to sit and enjoy traditional comfort in plush surroundings.

The inside has been refurbished in sympathy with the 17th century age of the building. The main door, leading from the garden at the side, opens into a large bar room where great bare stone pillars hold up a beamed ceiling. There are inglenooks and alcoves. Half-walls help divide the space up into separate 'rooms', so that customers can sit in quiet areas, away from the bar counter. Apart from the usual pub-style tables and chairs there are many armchairs and settees dotted around, giving a very homely feel. At the front of the building is a restaurant, also very comfortable.

As a freehouse the Trout Inn serves a range of drinks: real ales including Tanglefoot, Hook Norton, London Pride and Exmoor; draught cider (Blackthorn and Autumn Gold), and too many wines to mention. Teas, coffees and snacks are always available and the menus are comprehensive to say the least. Blackboards proclaim the daily specials. There are ploughman's lunches, sandwiches, jacket potatoes, things with chips, various fish courses, steaks and pies, vegetarian items and so on. The dessert counter displays a range of tempting cakes and sweets. The problem is what to choose. Perhaps you should ask the resident ghost for advice.

Telephone: 01884 855596.

How to get there: Bickleigh stands on the A396 road, along the Exe valley 4 miles south of Tiverton. It is just 10 miles north of Exeter city centre, and 5 miles west of Cullompton, where Junction 28 of the M5 motorway will be found. The Trout Inn stands on the western side of the A396, close to its junction with the A3072 road to Crediton.

Parking: There is a very large pub car park opposite, on the other side of the A396. Those also visiting the nearby 'Devonshire's Centre' at Bickleigh Mill may care to leave their vehicles in that car park instead. Cars should not be left on the busy main roads.

Length of the walk: 5½ miles. Map: OS Landranger sheet 192 Exeter and Sidmouth (inn GR 937077).

This is a long walk but a very easy one, since it uses clear gravel trackways and country lanes almost the whole way. It can also be shortened. There are no stiles to climb over, but there are some steep slopes to negotiate. Bickleigh Mill stands at a confluence, where the river Exe is joined by a number of tributary streams. This route goes along the valley of one of these streams, crosses over the hills through Cadeleigh village, and returns along the valley of another stream. Throughout the views are glorious across the rolling hills of North Devon.

The Walk
The route begins along the lane signposted to Cadeleigh, Upham and Cheriton Fitzpaine. To reach this turn right outside the Trout Inn and right again along the A3072 Crediton road. The lane to Cadeleigh will then be seen on the right.

But it would be a shame to leave Bickleigh before wandering around first. Over the bridge which crosses the river Exe is Bickleigh Mill where the 'Devonshire's Centre' offers all manner of tourist facilities. Apart from the old mill itself, there is an agricultural museum, fishing centre, 'birdland', a farm shop and various refreshment establishments. Behind this Centre, away from the main road, is Bickleigh village with its old cottages and 14th century church. Across the Exe valley, on the Trout Inn side of the river, is Bickleigh Castle.

Along the Cadeleigh lane you pass a thatched cottage on the right

114

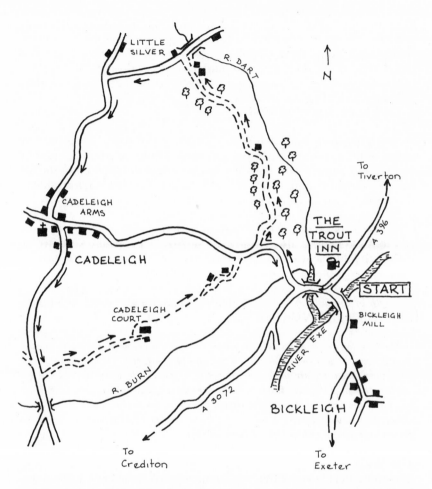

and begin to climb. The lane then bends to the left, and you will notice a stone wall to your right. At the end of this wall, before you have climbed too far along the lane, turn right, along an earthy trackway. This goes back a little and climbs between hedgebanks. This, effectively, is the beginning of your circular route.

The track curves to the left, levels off and continues through a gate, by this time as a grassy/stony trackway running under the trees. Down to the right, between the trees, you will see the valley of the river Dart – the stream you crossed back on the A3072 having left the Trout Inn. This, of course, is not the famous river Dart, that flows from Dartmoor to Dartmouth. This is a relatively small tributary of the Exe, flowing down from the hills around Witheridge.

115

For the next mile, a route description hardly seems necessary. The track winds a little, and goes up and down, but the way is clear throughout, as you follow the western side of the Dart valley up to Little Silver. For a short while you walk alongside the river, as it babbles amongst the trees, but later (after passing a single-storey stone cottage), you climb gradually upwards above the valley floor. Be sure to stop frequently, and admire the scenery.

A last dip, amongst a group of trees, followed by a walk past some cottages (called 'Upper Dart' and 'Ashilford'), brings you to the road at Little Silver. This is neither a village nor a hamlet, but a group of farmsteads dotted about the valley. On the road turn left, to walk steeply uphill, turning left again at the T-junction. This will bring you first to the farmstead of Yate, and then to the village of Cadeleigh.

This middle section of the route – for a distance of about 2 miles – is along a country lane, with tarmac underfoot. But it is a very quiet lane with grass in places growing down the middle.

Cadeleigh is a pretty, hilltop village with old cottages clustering around a road junction and a 15th century church. For those requiring refreshment the Cadeleigh Arms offers daylong service. Children are welcome, snacks are always available and cream teas are offered. Those wishing to shorten the walk can head eastwards from here, taking the road leading back to Bickleigh. Those wishing to continue the route as planned should take the lane opposite the Cadeleigh Arms, which leads south, past the post office. This is signposted to Cadbury – and indeed Cadbury Castle hill fort can now be seen on the skyline ahead. This is not the famous Cadbury Castle, of King Arthur associations. That one stands near Wincanton, in Somerset.

The lane goes steeply downhill. Towards the bottom, soon after it has curved to the left, a gravel track leads off to the left. This is signposted to Cadeleigh Court and is the beginning of the route back to Bickleigh. It is, in fact, the drive to Cadeleigh Court, but it is a public right of way as well. After winding around some fields the track reaches a high stone wall, at the edge of the Court's private gardens. Keep to the left and skirt the back of the buildings, keeping these to your right-hand side after bearing right. Two gates lead you between a couple of barns and thence the path crosses two fields. The way is clearly marked by arrow discs. Beyond the second field the path becomes a track again, running between hedgerows. All this way the valley of the river Burn should be down to your right.

The way back is clear. The track becomes a gravel, then a tarmac, lane as it bends round a farm and some old cottages. In due course you reach the road, where you turn right to descend back to Bickleigh. All the way the valley is down below on the right and beyond, on the far horizons, are the rolling hills of Devon.

28 Culmstock
The Ilminster Stage

This old, traditional coaching inn is now a popular, and equally traditional, village pub. The decor is unpretentious and the welcome is unaffected. The food is wholesome and excellent value, the beer is well-kept and the customers are obviously happy. What more could one ask of a local?

The Ilminster Stage has just one bar room, but it behaves like two. Upon entering, there is the public bar end, with dartboard, simple furniture and a bare floor. Sub-divided from this end by a half-screen is the part where stands the bar counter. This is evidently the lounge end, complete with carpet. At the rear of the building is a courtyard and beer garden. Families are welcome. Generally this pub keeps normal pub opening times, except on Saturdays, when it is open all day and Mondays, when it is closed at lunchtime.

This is a freehouse, serving such real ales as Worthington and the locally-brewed Otter. Draught cider and various wines are also offered. The regular menu, listing the usual pub fare, is supplemented by a blackboard with daily specials. The trout and steak meals are very good, as are the Sunday lunch roasts. Amongst the desserts old-fashioned English puddings prove popular, like jam roly-poly and spotted dick, both served with custard.

Telephone: 01884 840872.

How to get there: Culmstock stands at the western end of the Blackdown Hills, 11 miles east of Tiverton. Junction 27, on the M5 motorway, is just 3 miles away. Honiton is 10 miles to the south-east, Wellington 5 miles north-east, across the Somerset border. The Ilminster Stage will be found at the southern end of the village, opposite the church.

Parking: There is no pub car park but street parking outside is no problem – the village is very quiet.

Length of the walk: 5½ miles. Map: OS Landranger sheet 181 Minehead and Brendon Hills (inn GR 103135).

This walk is to Culmstock Beacon and back. Most of the route uses gravel lanes and farm tracks, so there should be no trouble finding the way. The short section that uses field paths, however, involves some stile climbing and a little dampness underfoot. The route also requires some effort up and down gradients.

Culmstock Beacon, which is topped by a beehive-shaped hut built for the burning of beacons, offers splendid views all around, northwards to the Quantocks and Exmoor, westwards towards Dartmoor. Culmstock village is worth a wander, having old and historic associations. Strolls along the river Culm may also be enjoyed.

The Walk

The route begins at the far end of Culmstock, so you must first walk through the village by turning left outside the pub and then right down Town Hill. This will give you a good opportunity to see something of this pleasant little place.

During the Middle Ages Culmstock was a thriving market town, with an important wool trade. But decline set in with the Industrial Revolution and the advent of cheap woollen cloth from Yorkshire. At about that time a railway line was built along the Culm valley, but this failed to prevent the settlement becoming something of a backwater. Today it is simply a large village possessing the last vestiges of industry – a large mill and a dismantled rail track. Accordingly it is a most charming, friendly spot. The 15th century church, intriguingly, has a tree growing out of its tower. Inside is a stained-glass window by the Pre-Raphaelite artist Burne-Jones. Down by the 14th century bridge over the Culm is the Culm Valley Inn, popular with tourists. Historians may be interested to know that Culmstock boasts two famous 19th century inhabitants – Frederick Temple who became Archbishop of Canterbury and RD Blackmore, author of *Lorna Doone*.

118

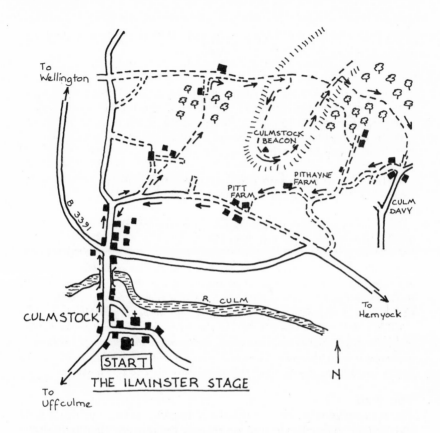

To Wellington

B 339I

CULMSTOCK BEACON

PITHAYNE FARM

PITT FARM

CULM DAVY

R. CULM

To Hemyock

CULMSTOCK

N

START

THE ILMINSTER STAGE

To Uffculme

Crossing the Culm bridge you continue northwards along a lane where the main road bends left, keeping the primary school to your immediate left and some housing estates to your right. Further on, close to a house called 'Fairlawn' a fork presents itself. Take the lane to the right, despite the fact that the lane to the left is signposted to Woodgate and, more interestingly, to the Beacon. That is the route cars would take. Shortly you do turn left, down a gravel track just past Knap House. The Beacon can be seen directly ahead.

Some 200 yards before the farm, which stands at the end of this track, climb the stile on the right and cross the field diagonally towards the Beacon. Another stile, and then a gate, take you across a farm trackway. Continue along the edge of the next field, with the hedge on your left. By this time you are gaining height so be sure to look behind: the views are spreading out. In the top corner a gate leads through to the only section of the entire walk that, depending upon season, can be difficult. The way is clear enough, being a path

119

running up between trees and hedges, but underfoot the ground could be damp and overgrown by nettles. Within a few hundred yards however you emerge from the trees, pass a house and reach a tarmac lane. The rest of the journey is easy, along well used trackways.

At the next junction, by a little house, turn right and begin the last ascent to the Beacon's summit. The tarmac gives way to gravel and, beyond a gate, the wide track climbs as it runs up beneath the trees. Soon you find heather, gorse and bracken either side and the top approaches. Shortly before the top turn right along another wide gravel track. This skirts the summit, keeping the steep slope down to your right-hand side. What a splendid section this is: a hilltop stroll with glorious views across Devon and Somerset. In due course you reach the Ordnance Survey Trig. Point and, close by, the circular beacon hut – the only one of its kind in Devon. In former times beacons like this were used to spread important news across England. The coming of the Spanish Armada for example was relayed across the country by such beacons. With the hole in the roof of this beacon hut it can easily be imagined, how a fire could be lit and its smoke sent aloft. Other summits would have had their own beacons, Dunkery on Exmoor for instance, and so messages could be sent across the land.

Continue along the track that keeps close to the edge, as it runs east and then north round the hilltop. It narrows slightly, to be more of a path, and accompanies a fence. In due course you reach a meeting of ways, the track left goes back to the summit, the track right descends next to a woodland. You, however, continue straight on, with the woodland to your right, and then – after about 300 yards – turn right through a metal farm gate. An attractive gravel track now takes you down beneath the beech trees. Passing a thatched cottage on the right you eventually emerge down at Culm Davy hamlet and the tarmac road. Turn right, and immediately right again along a narrow lane hemmed in by hedgerows. This curves past some cottages. Keep right at the next fork (along a lane marked 'Unsuitable for Motors') and then left at the next T-junction. After the next left bend turn right along a grassy, rutted track to Pithayne Farm.

The right of way actually runs through that farm's garden and then left but, naturally, the farmer prefers walkers to go through the gate to the left of the garden and skirt the top of the adjoining field. Keeping the farm buildings to your right you now cross the field diagonally to a stile and then, in the same direction, cross the next field to a gate. Now bearing slightly left you aim to the left of Pitt Farm, where you reach a farm lane. Turn right, to follow this lane all the way back to the northern end of Culmstock. But take your time. This is lovely countryside and the views across the Culm valley, over to the left, should not be ignored.

Kentisbeare
Keepers Cottage Inn

This certainly has the feel of an old cottage which has been converted into an inn. Inside there are bare stone walls and small rooms where domestic furniture and decor give a very homely atmosphere. A piano stands in one corner. There is one main bar room but other sitting areas lead off from here, where families and diners tend to congregate. To the left is a lounge-type room, to the right (behind the large fireplace) is a restaurant-type room. In winter months a log fire burns in the hearth and the place is very cosy indeed.

The Keepers Cottage is a freehouse, serving real ales including Bass and Otter, Dry Blackthorn cider and a wide selection of wines. There is a good choice of food ranging from bar snacks to main meals. Amongst the former are ploughman's lunches and variously filled sandwiches; amongst the latter are meat pies, fish dishes and salads. Vegetarians are offered three different snack items and five different main meals – so there should be something here they like. The chips are very good and the pastry is excellent.

Normal pub opening times are kept. Children are very welcome and the garden contains various items of children's play equipment including a climbing frame and swings. This is a friendly, welcoming place and, not surprisingly, has become very popular.

Telephone: 01884 266247.

How to get there: The Keepers Cottage Inn does not, in fact, stand in the village of Kentisbeare, which is 1 mile away. It stands on the A373 road 3 miles east of Cullompton and 7 miles north-west of Honiton. Junction 28 of the M5 motorway is little more than 2 miles distant. Here, we are on the western edge of the Blackdown Hills.

Parking: There is a large pub car park. Vehicles should not be left along the A373 except in the lay-by opposite the Keepers Cottage. Space may also be found in some of the country lanes leading off on either side.

Length of the walk: 3½ miles. Map: OS Landranger sheet 192 Exeter and Sidmouth (inn GR 064067).

This route uses quiet country lanes, farm tracks and footpaths across fields. It is undemanding: there are no steep gradients, and no difficulties in pathfinding. Some stiles and gates must be climbed however and some field corners may be muddy after wet weather. The views are pleasant throughout.

The walk crosses the valley of the river Weaver (an upper tributary of the river Culm) and includes the villages of Dulford and Kerswell. Those wishing to lengthen the distance, or else undertake other walks from the Keepers Cottage Inn, may like to walk up North Hill (east of Kerswell) from where expansive views may be enjoyed.

The Walk

The route begins through the woods immediately behind the Keepers Cottage Inn. There is a footpath signpost by the roadside and this points the way, and a concrete plank bridge takes you over a ditch into the forest. Truth to tell the exact path is difficult to follow. There are many little paths that wander between the trees and this network can be confusing. The easiest way through lies along the path that winds close to the northern edge of the wood. Keep the open fields in sight through the trees to your right. In due course you reach a wide grassy track, or forest ride. Follow this to the left. At the far end a gate leads out to the road.

Across this road take the lane that leads to Daisyford and the Dulford Nurseries. This is a tarmac lane, but narrow with a hedgerow either side. At the Nurseries it ends but a grassy, rutted track continues at the far side of the yard, which you reach by keeping the house and buildings to your right. This track curves down beneath some trees eventually to meet a country lane. Turn right. You now follow this

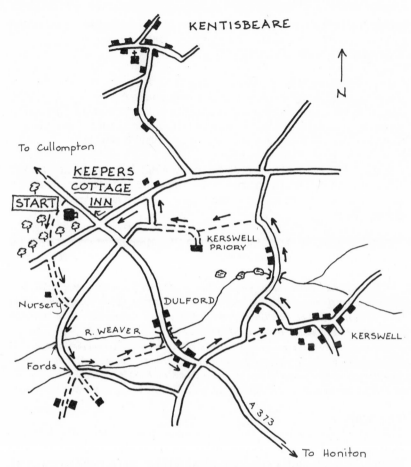

lane for a short distance as it curves down to a ford (where you can use a footbridge) and then up to another little ford (where you can use a plank bridge). At the junction where you cross the second ford keep left. The lanes to the right and straight on, although tarmac covered, are farm roads and, as such, dead ends.

There are pleasant views all round now. To the left and ahead are the Blackdowns, with the wooded slopes of North Hill dominating the skyline. The valley that you have just crossed is that of the river Weaver, which flows into the river Culm near Bradninch, 4 miles away south-westwards. The rivulet you crossed at the second ford, and which accompanies the lane for a short while along this stretch, is a tributary of the Weaver – a side channel once used by Dulford Mill, which you will pass in due course.

As the lane bears right, amongst some trees, a footpath signpost will be seen pointing left, over a plank footbridge and a stile. Once over these, and into the field, you turn right to cross the corner to another stile. The rivulet is still close by, flowing across the grass. Along the edge of the next two fields, keeping the hedge to your right and the Weaver valley down to your left, you eventually meet a gate. Beyond this, a clear path leads past some houses to the road. Turn right. This is the village of Dulford, its old mill being seen on the other side of the road. The waterfall, once operating the waterwheel, still flows down one side of the building.

Keeping to the pavement follow the road (in fact, the A373) up and out of the village. At the crossroads where stands an old red telephone box, turn left along a narrow lane. Further up, where this lane bends sharply left, continue in the same direction across the fields. A footpath signpost here points the way along a line of trees. Be sure to turn round along this stretch. On clear days the Dartmoor skyline can be seen. At the far end a stile, which is half-hidden in the hedgerow, takes you into the next field. Here you aim diagonally, towards North Hill which rises in the distance. Soon you meet a hedgerow which you accompany down towards the houses of Kerswell village. Do not, however, go all the way down to these houses. On the left, a stile leads through the hedgerow you have been following. This takes you, rather curiously, around the perimeter of a private garden. Keeping to the top edge of this you find a path that leads down between some bungalows to the road. Turn left, unless of course you wish to look around the village. In this case go straight on and return to this point later.

Leaving Kerswell behind, you reach a T-junction, where you turn right, in the Kentisbeare direction. This lane dips and curves left as it passes a couple of houses and offers a view (to the left) of a lake. This is one of a small group created by the damming of the upper Weaver. Continue along the lane as it rises out of the valley to a right-hand bend. At this point turn left and follow the direction indicated by the footpath signpost. Along the edge of a field you reach a gate beyond which (over a stile) you reach a gravel track. This leads left to Kerswell Priory and right to the road. Follow the latter course. The landscape hereabouts appears, at one time, to have been designed into a 'parkland', with trees dotted around. The lakes mentioned earlier also indicate this. The fields roundabout evidently once formed part of the Kerswell Priory estate.

In due course you reach the road. Turn right. At the next T-junction turn left. The main road is soon reached, and (to the right) the Keepers Cottage Inn.

Fenny Bridges
The Fenny Bridges Inn

This is a popular stopping place for those driving to and from Cornwall along the A30. It is large, friendly and serves an excellent range of food and drink. But it is also popular amongst locals, and people come here from nearby Exeter and Honiton.

This Georgian building has been pleasantly refurbished inside, with modern yet tasteful decor. The carpets and wallpaper give the rooms a plush look, and the cushioned, pink-and-grey chairs are comfortable. On the walls hang pictures of country scenes and dotted about the floors are tall pot plants. The main open-plan bar room has one end which is set aside as a dining area and another which acts as a lounge. To one side, is a separate public bar complete with pool table.

This is a freehouse serving various real ales (including John Smith's and locally brewed Otter bitter), Blackthorn cider and a selection of mainly French wines. The food selection is listed on menu books and on display blackboards. The choice ranges from bar snacks to full-blown meals, from special children's dishes to vegetarian items. There are jacket potatoes, open sandwiches and home-made soups; there are grills, pies, pasties and fish platters; there are things with chips, vegetable risottos, samosas and pancakes. The evening meals are very popular and special cuisine nights are held.

Normal pub opening times are kept, children are welcome and there is a garden at the rear. Children will be especially intrigued by the old well, now glass-covered, that stands next to the lounge bar counter. Telephone: 01404 850218.

How to get there: Fenny Bridges stands on the A30 trunk road just 3 miles west of Honiton and 2 miles north of Ottery St Mary. The village is situated on the river Otter, at the south-western edge of the Blackdown Hills. The inn will be found on the north side of the main road.

Parking: There is a large car park at the rear and a few cars can also be left at the front of the pub. In addition, there is a gravel area opposite, which belongs to the inn, and this can also be used for parking. This means that, in whichever direction you are heading, you can park without first having to cross the line of traffic. This is a big advantage, for the A30 can be very busy indeed.

Length of the walk: 4½ miles. Map: OS Landranger sheet 192 Exeter and Sidmouth (inn GR 113985).

This walk goes to Westgate Hill and back. The outward journey is by way of a clear bridleway, the return journey is along country lanes, farm tracks and footpaths across fields. The route is clear throughout. Some stiles must be negotiated however and the ground underfoot can be soft due to the churning of horses' hooves.

This is a lovely corner of Devon and there are views to be had across the Otter valley to the higher parts of the Blackdowns. The top of Westgate Hill is wooded, with patches of moorland vegetation, thus offering very pleasant walking country.

The Walk

From outside the Fenny Bridges Inn walk eastwards along the busy A30, in the Honiton direction. Fortunately you do not stay on this road for long. After crossing the river Otter by way of the second bridge – the older one made of stone – turn immediately right, along a public bridleway. This firm-surfaced path curves up between bushes, eventually to reach the B3177 at the eastern end of Alfington. Here you cross straight over to a gate, where a bridleway signpost points the way uphill. Follow the direction indicated. Keeping the hedgerow on your left proceed along the edges of two fields, until a couple of farm gates lead you through to a grassy trackway. This continues in the same direction, running between hedgerows and aiming directly for the wooded slopes of Westgate Hill.

The route is very clear. The track rises gradually and is fairly

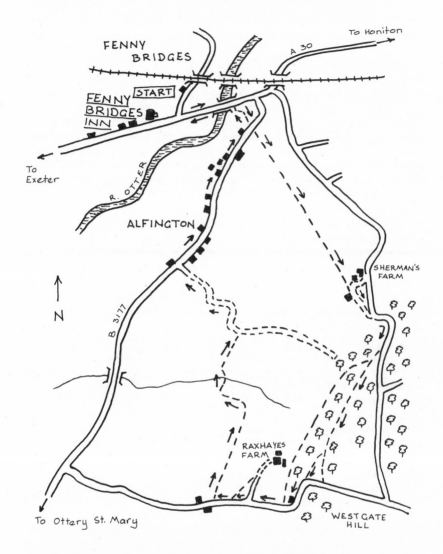

FENNY
BRIDGES

To Honiton

A 30

START

FENNY
BRIDGES
INN

To
Exeter

R. OTTER

ALFINGTON

N

B 3/77

SHERMAN'S
FARM

RAXHAYES
FARM

To Ottery St. Mary

WESTGATE
HILL

straight. Beyond Sherman's Farm (which is half-hidden from view by the hedgerow on your left) and a thatched cottage on your right, the surface underfoot becomes gravel and shingle. Along this stretch be sure to look around – and especially behind – for the views begin to open out. Down below is the Otter valley. Beyond and northwards are the green slopes of the Blackdown Hills. It is hard to imagine that this was the scene of a bloody battle. But in 1549, during the reign of the boy King Edward VI, it was indeed the place where many perished. A West Country revolt, led by the Cornishmen, was finally put down by the Lord Protector's forces. It had begun in opposition to the new Prayer Book, but developed into a general uprising against social oppression and agricultural reorganisation. The battle field itself was west of Honiton, not far from Fenny Bridges.

Towards the top a sharp left bend brings the gravel track to the road. Turn right and continue uphill through the woods. Round the next hairpin bend the road begins to level off. Along this stretch turn right to follow a grassy trackway that runs at an angle through the trees. After about 50 yards another trackway leads off to the right but you ignore this. Continue in the same direction (southwards) and soon you will find yourself walking through an open clearing. The trees give way to gorse and the vegetation becomes distinctly moorland in character. In summer the heather makes for a colourful sight.

At a fork keep to the right, to follow a trackway more stony than the previous one. Continue along this, ignoring other tracks either side, until you reach a wide gravel track that joins from the left. Bear right and follow this as it descends, curving down along the edge of the woodland. Close to a large house this track becomes a tarmac lane. Keeping the house to your right proceed down this lane. The views are now ahead: westward towards central Devon.

In due course the lane passes the entrance drive to Raxhayes Farm (on the right) and then a footpath signpost (also on the right). It then passes another farm and curves right. At this point another footpath signpost points right. This is the route to follow. Beyond the stile and gate here the path leads up across a field to the trees on the skyline. Beyond these continue in the same direction, keeping alongside a wire fence. Aiming for the valley ahead you soon find yourself accompanyng a hedgerow on your left. Just before reaching the stream a stile in this hedgerow leads you through to the next field. Follow the bottom edge of this, until – in the far corner – you dip down to the right to cross the stream. There is no bridge here but the stream is shallow and narrow so there should be little difficulty in reaching the far side. Up the grassy slope a stile will be found beneath the trees. Beyond this a grassy trackway leads you onward, between hedges and through some shrubland. At the top a gate and stile take you onto a wide sandy track. Turn left.

The way back is now very easy. Follow this track all the way to Alfington village, which you reach at its western end nearly opposite the Alfington Inn. Turn right, to walk along the road all the way through the village. It is a straggling place but some of the cottages are old and interesting. Beyond the very last cottage on the left ('Beaumont Cottage') turn left down the bridleway signposted. This is the one you followed at the start. The Fenny Bridges Inn beckons.